T0318833

THE NATIONAL INSTITUTE OF
ECONOMIC AND SOCIAL RESEARCH

Economic and Social Studies
XIV

BRITISH
ECONOMIC STATISTICS

2 DEAN TRENCH STREET, SMITH SQUARE
LONDON, S.W. I

The National Institute of Economic and Social Research is an independent, non-profit-making body founded in 1938. It always has had as its aim the promotion of realistic research, particularly in the field of economics. It conducts research by its own research staff and in co-operation with the Universities and other academic bodies. The results of the work done under the Institute's auspices are published in several series, and a list of its publications up to the present time will be found at the end of this book.

BRITISH ECONOMIC STATISTICS

A REPORT

BY

C. F. CARTER

AND

A. D. ROY

CAMBRIDGE

AT THE UNIVERSITY PRESS

1954

CAMBRIDGE
UNIVERSITY PRESS

University Printing House, Cambridge CB2 8BS, United Kingdom

Cambridge University Press is part of the University of Cambridge.

It furthers the University's mission by disseminating knowledge in the pursuit of education, learning and research at the highest international levels of excellence.

www.cambridge.org
Information on this title: www.cambridge.org/9781316603888

© Cambridge University Press 1954

First published 1954
First paperback edition 2015

A catalogue record for this publication is available from the British Library

ISBN 978-1-316-60388-8 Paperback

Cambridge University Press has no responsibility for the persistence or accuracy of URLs for external or third-party internet websites referred to in this publication, and does not guarantee that any content on such websites is, or will remain, accurate or appropriate.

CONTENTS

LIST OF TABLES

PREFACE

The origin of this report is explained in Chapter 1. We wrote it, and its errors and shortcomings are ours; but the Committee of the National Institute which directed the project was a 'working committee' of experts with experience in the Government service, and they gave us not only general guidance but a great deal of detailed assistance. We were helped, too, by academic colleagues in many universities, and by statisticians in industry, in international agencies, and in the statistical services of the United States of America, Canada, and the Republic of Ireland. Above all, we are grateful to the many British Government statisticians who have borne patiently with our questionings, and who have given us all the information we required. We hope we may have been able in some small measure to repay their kindness by drawing attention to the difficulty and importance of their work.

C. F. CARTER
The Queen's University, Belfast

A. D. ROY
Sidney Sussex College, Cambridge

May 1953

References in square brackets, thus: [**26**],
refer to the bibliography at the end.

CHAPTER I

INTRODUCTION

The origin of this inquiry was a decision of the Executive Committee of the National Institute of Economic and Social Research, in November 1950, to initiate a project called 'An Examination of British Economic Statistics'. This was to have, as its main object,

> 'the investigation of the statistical information (a) required for, or (b) actually used or available for, the formulation of economic policy in the United Kingdom.'

Economic policy was to be understood in a general sense—covering such things as employment policy or fiscal policy; the inquiry was not to concern itself with statistics needed solely for detailed administrative decisions. It was to be a review and assessment of existing statistics, and also an investigation of the statistical requirements for the formulation of policy.

Fifty years ago[1] there were no production statistics outside a few staples, such as coal, pig iron and steel. International trade was reasonably well covered, and estimates could be made of the British consumption of commodities such as cotton, wool and wheat, of which a good part passed through the ports. The basic financial and fiscal statistics were published; wage rates were known for selected trades, and unemployment figures could be obtained from Trade Union returns. Indices of wholesale prices were available, and there was some scattered information about retail prices, mainly of food. General 'activity' could be seen reflected in the railway returns, the shipping clearances, or the bank clearings. But the items of this rudimentary statistical system were often of an unsatisfactory kind; thus the 'consumption' of raw wool was obtained by adding retained imports to the retained domestic clip, and ignored stock (inventory) changes. If one tries to extend a 'modern' statistical series back to the beginning of the century, all sorts of difficulties arise—a good example is provided by Dr A. R. Prest's description of his preliminary estimates of national income for the period 1870 to 1914.[2]

By 1939 things were substantially better; the *Guide to Current Official Statistics of the United Kingdom*,[3] published annually from 1922, gives an

---

[1] The position a little earlier, in 1885, was described by Dr (later Sir) Robert Giffen to the Royal Commission on the Depression of Trade and Industry: see [95].
[2] Prest [110]. [3] [23].

idea of the wealth of information available. But the user was still faced by difficulties of inadequate coverage, of varying classification, and so on, and many areas of statistics now familiar were hardly developed at all. In the field of industrial production, for instance, the Board of Trade index of 1935 contained about 85 series; the Central Statistical Office index of 1952 contains 1,300. In 1939 national income statistics of a simple kind had been worked out by a few private investigators: in 1952 the extensive and complex information given in the National Income White Papers draws from the resources of almost every Government department, and forms a considerable part of the work of the Central Statistical Office. The information available on the Balance of Payments, though it is still (as we shall see in Chapter VIII) in some ways confusing and incomplete, is incomparably better than the scanty estimates of 1939. In many other fields there has been a great increase of statistical knowledge, not only in the United Kingdom but throughout the world.

This change has not been uniform; some types of statistics have been developed almost to excess, while for others there may have been some retrogression. The growth of statistical information was, in fact, haphazard.[1] Much of it came into being in response to some special administrative need, perhaps short-lived; some of the streams of facts coming in in this way have been diverted and 'treated' to adapt them for other uses. Co-ordination has grown, but this too has been a response to the needs of the moment. It seemed therefore useful that, after this period of growth, someone should take a general view of the whole subject. In deciding to attempt this, the National Institute realized that the Central Statistical Office would naturally, as part of its work, be keeping a watchful eye on the development of the statistical system. But it would not have been easy for the C.S.O., which is a user as well as a co-ordinator of statistics, and which is heavily burdened with its day-to-day work, to free personnel for the whole task which the Institute had in mind. There seemed to be a case here for using the resources and the wide range of contacts of a non-official body.

THE COMMITTEE AND ITS METHODS

The plan of research followed the Institute's usual pattern: research workers (in this case the two authors, part-time) under the direction of a Committee. The Committee was not merely to decide the general policy of the inquiry, but to take an active part in it; and all of its members had themselves spent periods in the Government service, and knew at first hand the problem of providing a statistical basis for policy-making. The membership was:

[1] Though a scheme for development appears in the 1944 White Paper on *Employment Policy* [58].

PROFESSOR R. G. D. ALLEN, O.B.E., M.A., D.Sc. (Econ.) (Chairman)

Professor of Statistics, University of London, since 1944: Assistant Lecturer and later Lecturer in Statistics, London School of Economics, 1928–39: Reader in Economic Statistics, University of London, 1939–44: Statistician, H.M. Treasury, 1939–41: Director of Records and Statistics, British Supply Council, Washington, 1941–2: British Director of Research and Statistics, Combined Production and Resources Board, Washington, 1942–5: Statistical Adviser, H.M. Treasury, 1947–8: Consultant, United Nations Statistical Office, 1949–50.

PROFESSOR A. K. CAIRNCROSS, C.M.G., M.A., Ph.D.

Professor of Applied Economics, University of Glasgow, since 1951: Lecturer, 1935–9: Civil Servant—Offices of the War Cabinet, 1940–1; Board of Trade, 1941; Ministry of Aircraft Production, 1941–5; Director of Programmes, Ministry of Aircraft Production, 1945; Economic Advisory Panel, Berlin, 1945–6; Economic Adviser to the Board of Trade, 1946–9: Economic Adviser to the Organisation for European Economic Co-operation, Paris, 1949–50.

PROFESSOR E. DEVONS, M.A.

Robert Ottley Professor of Applied Economics, University of Manchester, since 1948: Economic Assistant, Joint Committee of Cotton Trade Organisations, 1935–9: Statistician, Cotton Control, Ministry of Supply, 1939–40: Statistician, Economic Section of the Offices of the War Cabinet and later Chief Statistician, Central Statistical Office, 1940–1: successively Chief Statistician, Director of Statistics, Director-General of Planning, Programmes and Statistics, Ministry of Aircraft Production, 1941–5: Reader in Economic Statistics, University of Manchester, 1945–8.

SIR DONALD MACDOUGALL, C.B.E., M.A. (Kt.cr. 1953)

Fellow of Nuffield College, Oxford, since 1947: Nuffield Reader in International Economics, Oxford University, since 1951: Assistant and later Lecturer in Economics, University of Leeds, 1936–9: First Lord of the Admiralty's Statistical Branch, 1939–40: Prime Minister's Statistical Branch, 1940–5 (Chief Assistant, 1942–5): Fellow of Wadham College, Oxford, 1945–50: Lecturer in Economics, University of Oxford, 1947–51: Economics Director, Organisation for European Economic Co-operation, Paris, 1948–9.

(Sir Donald resigned from the Committee in November 1951, when he joined the Prime Minister's Statistical Section. He was therefore not present at the discussion of this report.)

W. B. REDDAWAY, M.A.

Fellow of Clare College, Cambridge since 1938: Lecturer in Economics, University of Cambridge, since 1939: Assistant, Bank of England, 1934–5: Research Fellow in Economics, University of Melbourne, 1936–7: Statistics Division, Board of Trade, 1940–7 (final rank Chief Statistician): Economic Adviser to the Organisation for European Economic Co-operation, Paris, 1951–2.

RICHARD STONE, C.B.E., M.A.

Director, Department of Applied Economics, and Fellow, King's College, Cambridge since 1945: with C. E. Heath and Co., Lloyd's Brokers, 1936–9: Ministry of Economic Warfare, 1939–40: Offices of the War Cabinet, Central Statistical Office, 1940–5: Director, National Accounts Research Unit, O.E.E.C., 1949–52, and subsequently Consultant to the Directorate of Statistics and National Accounts of that Organisation: Consultant, Statistical Office of the United Nations, 1952: Visiting Professor in Political Economy, The Johns Hopkins University, 1953.

The Committee met first at the end of November 1950, and mapped out a programme of interviews with statisticians in Government departments and with important users of British economic statistics, such as the London and Cambridge Economic Service and the Economic Co-operation Administration (later the Mutual Security Agency) of the United States of America. In February 1951 a letter was sent to a number of academic economists and industrial statisticians, asking for their help in suggesting points for investigation; numerous helpful replies were received. Interviews continued throughout 1951 and early 1952, and the Committee at its meetings (of which there were eleven in all) considered the results of these, and successive outlines and preliminary drafts of a report. A complete draft, prepared in the autumn of 1952, was submitted for comments to a number of Government statisticians. This enabled us to correct a number of errors of fact and emphasis, but those consulted are, of course, in no way responsible for what we have written, nor do we expect that this report carries their full agreement.

RELATIONSHIP TO OTHER INQUIRIES

Our task was made much simpler by the fact that we decided not to attempt a description of the statistics of the United Kingdom. The Royal Statistical Society is publishing, in its *Journal* (*Series A*), descriptive articles about the statistics available on particular subjects; their net is cast widely, to bring in industrial and some foreign statistics, as well as those of Government origin. A first batch of twenty of these articles was republished in book form[1] in 1952. Certain descriptive guides to departmental statistics have been published by the Inter-departmental Committee on Social and Economic Research (commonly known as the North Committee, after its Chairman, Dr George North, C.B., M.C., Head of the General Register Office). The first of these, on Labour Statistics,[2] was published in 1948 and revised in 1950; the second, on Census Reports of Great Britain, 1801–1931,[3] appeared in 1951. The intention was, apparently, that there should be a series which would collectively act as a successor to the pre-war *Guides to Current Official Statistics*, but with much fuller information; progress has, how-ever, been disappointingly slow.[4]

We could therefore aim at an appraisal, not at a description. We did not search systematically for parallel work in overseas countries, but there is one overseas investigation which should clearly be mentioned here. This is an investigation undertaken in the United States in 1948 for the Commission on Organization of the Executive Branch of the Government, the 'Hoover Commission'. The authors were Professors Frederick C. Mills and Clarence D. Long, then working with the National Bureau of Economic Research; their assignment was to prepare, within about six months, a survey of Federal statistical agencies. The resulting report[5] is naturally largely concerned with organizational problems; but it covers much of the ground which we shall try to cover below, and we had frequent occasion to refer to it.

A previous report in the same field was that on Government Statistics, produced by a joint Committee of the American Statistical Association and the Social Science Research Council, 1933–5, and published by the Social Science Research Council in 1937. The American Statistical Association has a standing Committee on Statistical Standards and Organization, and in 1951 the Association reported that it had organized an Advisory Committee on Statistical Policy to the Division[6] of Statistical Standards, Bureau of the Budget. This latter committee, composed of past presidents of the A.S.A. and with the late E. A. Goldenweiser as first Chairman, was to advise the Division 'on broad matters of public policy in the statistical area'.[7] It first turned its attention to the problem of confidentiality of individual statistical returns, which we discuss below (Chapter XI).

---

[1] [102].   [2] [66].   [3] [54].

[4] Reference may also be made to the Central Statistical Office series, *Studies in Official Statistics*. The first two volumes [62, 62a] both relate to the indices of industrial production.

[5] *The Statistical Agencies of the Federal Government* [106].   [6] Now 'Office'.

[7] *The American Statistician*, vol. 5, no. 4, October 1951, p. 2; vol. 6, no. 2, April 1952, p. 10 [118].

DEFINING THE FIELD OF INVESTIGATION

The Committee found it necessary at an early stage to give careful thought to the right interpretation of its terms of reference. First of all, what does one mean by the 'use' of statistics in policy-making? A decision made in the Cabinet, in an official Committee or in a Government office may rest on an agreed rational assessment of facts, including statistical facts. It may equally be a compromise between opposed points of view, or it may be founded on the intuitions of a dominant personality, or upon an idea of what Parliament or the public expect or will tolerate. Every statistician knows how easy it is, by appropriate selection, to give statistical 'proofs' of contradictory points of view. It must be expected, therefore, that sometimes a policy decision not backed by any agreed rational argument will be dressed with a statistical justification. Occasionally, also, a façade of statistics may conceal an absence of policy—the statistics suggesting by their presence a scientific use of facts which is not in reality being made. We think that there may be some danger of this in the field of location policy.

The genuine use of statistics in the formulation of policy cannot therefore be taken as identical with the input of statistics into policy-making agencies. It would be interesting to examine the process of policy-making in some typical instances: to trace, for instance, the links of reasoning which join the facts of the Balance of Payments to a decision to make specific import cuts. But clearly such an examination is quite impossible. Even if one could listen to the process of policy-making when it takes place behind closed doors, it is doubtful if one could unravel the various strands which go into the making of a decision. The mechanical analogy, which regards statistics as the input into a machine whose final product is neatly packeted decisions, is a false one. The same policy decision can be reached by various ways and different people will reach it by different paths. Even within the mind of one policy-maker, various and perhaps inconsistent reasons for and against a given course of action will contend for acceptance, and once the decision is made it will often be difficult, even for the policy-maker himself, to recall the subtle balance of argument which led to it. We shall not usually be able to reconstruct that argument by studying only the reasons given in public justification for the decision.

We admit, therefore, the intrinsic difficulty of reaching decisions in the complexity of economic life—and the virtual impossibility of unravelling them, once made. But it remains true that an important part of the process of policy-making employs numerical facts or makes deductions from economic relations of a mathematical kind. It is with this simplified and partial aspect of policy-making that we are concerned.

We do not suggest that decisions can or should be reached solely in this way; but we do claim that the type of argument which employs statistics is important, perhaps increasingly important, to the development of British economic policy today.

Our difficulties do not end here. What are the 'policies' whose statistical basis we are examining? Will they not alter as one party or another provides the Government? Will not the statistical requirements of independent experts who wish to assess policy be as various as their opinions and prejudices?

There is, of course, a large range of basic statistics which will be required by any modern state, in order that a watch may be kept on changes in the economy. But the elaboration and frequency of the information needed depend a good deal on the nature of the policies it is required to serve—in particular, on the choice (if it exists) between physical controls and a free price mechanism. Some of the wartime growth of statistics was not merely an administrative by-product of controls; the statistics themselves found their main use in guiding the operation of the controls, and (in a free market) might appropriately be collected in quite a different form. An example is the Board of Trade index of utility-furniture production. Again, the nature of the information gathered depends on the relative importance given to current decision and to historical study. The needs of the moment may require one form of statistics, comparison with past periods another.

It is interesting to note that Mills and Long[1] give no attention to this difficulty, although they recognize that the willingness of Congress to finance statistical investigations, or of the public to submit to them, is not limitless. They seem to assume a tacit agreement about what is needed. This country is a long way from being able to spare time, men and money to collect and publish all the figures which might reasonably be wanted, now or in the future; a choice has to be made, and it seems to us that there are bound to be differences of view about how it should be made. Our own endeavour must be to keep to a middle path.

We have therefore tried to interpret the words 'statistical information required for...the formation of economic policy' in a broad and reasonable manner. We have perhaps assumed of our ideal policy-makers more adherence to economic principle than their real-life counterparts can be supposed to possess; and we have done our best to bear in mind the needs of different schools of economic and political thought, and of long-term study by the historians.

[1] [106].

THE PLAN OF THE BOOK

A list of possible economic decisions, with the statistics required for each of them, would be tedious and could hardly be comprehensive. A list of existing economic statistics, each examined in relation to their possible uses, would not draw attention to the matters of fundamental interest. (A reference table of the principal British economic statistics and their sources will be found at the end of the book.) The approach we have used is a mixed one. Chapter II sets out some of the points of principle which seem, *a priori*, to be important, while Chapter III is a preview of the problems which are illustrated by the case-studies of Chapters IV–IX. The last of these, Chapter IX, examines the relation of statistics to a very general field of policy—namely, that arising from the assumption by the State of an obligation to preserve a right balance of aggregate supply and demand, and between the country and the rest of the world.

The lessons of these chapters, foreshadowed in Chapter III, are examined and discussed in Chapters X–XII under the general headings of Quality, Presentation and Organization. Chapter XIII shows the main conclusions to which our inquiry has led us.

CHAPTER II

STATISTICS AND ECONOMIC POLICY

We have already pointed out[1] that the relation between statistics and policy may be partial, obscure, and difficult to trace; and that when a country is developing a statistical *system*, it will need to have in mind the needs of differing policy-makers in varied future circumstances. But now we need to think more carefully about the nature of the help which numerical facts can give in developing or guiding policy.

A policy is a *course* of action; that is to say, something which runs through a period of time, during which there is repeated application of the principles or rules defined or implicit in the policy. These repeated applications are the individual 'administrative' or 'executive' decisions, of which millions are made in Government offices each year; a typical instance would be a decision to allocate Messrs A.B. ten tons of steel. Such a decision may be the automatic result of applying a precise rule, or it may involve considerable judgement in interpreting policy. Unless this judgement influences future decisions (for example, by 'creating a precedent') we may class the decision as concerned with administration and not with policy. A considerable apparatus of statistics—what might be called 'operating statistics'—is needed to keep a check on administrative action. Thus if allocations of steel add up to much more than the amount of steel available, this provides some evidence that the machinery of allocation has gone wrong.

We are not directly concerned with these 'operating statistics', though, as we shall show, they can often be diverted and made to serve wider purposes. Policy itself may employ statistics in three quite distinct ways. The first is to provide the background of facts into which the policy is fitted; the second is to elaborate implications, to set out the results which will or may flow from the operation of a possible policy; the third, to indicate how a policy already adopted is working. In order to decide a course of action in a complex and interconnected economy it will usually be necessary to simplify—to ignore distant and tenuous connexions and small indirect effects, and to concentrate on a few essentials. In the terminology of the econometricians, the policy-maker will employ a *model*—a simplified mental picture of the way in which the elements essential to his problem are related to each other.

There will be different ways of selecting what is essential, and differences of view about the relations of the essential elements. This is

[1] P. 6 above.

especially natural, because a policy is designed to run over some future period, and is affected by all the uncertainties of the future. There will be possible variations in expectations about future events. The 'parameters' of the models—that is to say, numbers which define numerical interconnections in them—will, to a greater or less degree, be subject to this uncertainty. It is here that statistics have their first function; by summarizing certain aspects of the experience of the past, they help to establish probabilities for the future. They limit the range within which it is reasonable to expect the parameters of the models to lie—or, to look at the matter another way, they exclude certain models, certain mental pictures of the problem, from practical consideration. But it is important to realize that there are many non-statistical problems of policy, and that even where statistics can help they cannot finally decide the choice of model on which the policy decision is to be based. There are three reasons for this: the necessary uncertainty of the future; the element of choice involved in deciding how to simplify a problem; and the usual inadequacies and uncertainties of the statistics themselves.

Suppose now that the mental picture is already drawn. Then it may be possible to use statistics to elaborate the implications of a particular policy. Chapter IX is in effect an example of this process, in which past experience, and expectations and assumptions about the future, are brought together into estimates of the size and use of the national product for the coming year. These estimates can be varied to take account of the results of alternative policy decisions—for example, different changes in taxation. Some of these policies will then be seen to set up strains and stresses in the system—shown in this case by an inconsistency in the interlocking set of social accounts—and the further results of these strains (for example, an inflation of prices, or a deficit on overseas accounts) may be predictable.

The first use of statistics may help to exclude from consideration certain ideas of reality, and therefore certain policies; the second helps the policy-maker to make a choice between the reasonable policies, by showing in a numerical form results likely to flow from each. When a choice has been made, statistics have a third important function to perform—to throw light on the success or failure of the policy, and to give timely warning of a change in circumstances which may render necessary a change in policy. Thus the success of the policies aimed at general balance in the economy, discussed in Chapter IX, would be judged by the course of prices, industrial production, imports and exports, consumption, retail trade and so forth.

But, as in the first use, so in the second and third it is important not to claim too much for what statistics may achieve. There are many aspects of policy-making other than those which can be put in a numerical form; there are many policies whose success or failure cannot be judged solely by numerical measures. There is a very real danger of claiming too much precision and relevance for econometric methods— a claim which tends to discredit them with those who have to make decisions. One aspect of this danger is that not enough attention is given to the inherent uncertainty of the future;[1] a deterministic or mechanical model, employing precise assumptions about what will happen in a coming period, may suggest a policy which is rigid and unsuited to meet the shocks of circumstance.

THE HISTORICAL DEVELOPMENT

Until modern times most economic action by the State has either had no numerical foundation, or has used a few statistical scraps which in themselves were an inadequate basis. But we must except from this those things capable of regulation by keeping money accounts. Accounting figures are a kind of statistics—in fact, of course, much the most important kind in determining the economic 'policies' of business firms and of individuals. Some non-financial statistical knowledge has existed from the earliest times—King David's unpopular effort to number his people[2] was not the first example—but a period of rapid development and of heightened interest in statistics did not come until 1790–1850. This period saw the foundation of several of the great statistical societies, and a flood of papers, mostly describing the social and economic conditions of the time.

The century since 1850 has seen slow additions to knowledge, the acceptance by Government of many more statistical responsibilities,[3] and (since 1900) a rapid development of the mathematical theory of the subject. We are now in the middle of a second period of growth and of heightened interest in statistical matters; thus, the membership of the Royal Statistical Society has doubled since 1939. Much of the use of statistics in this latest period has been a development and improvement of what has been done before; but there has also been a change of emphasis. If, as in the nineteenth century, the economic system is considered to be largely self-regulating, and especially if such State intervention as exists follows conventions (such as the convention of a balanced budget), the main function of statistics must be to provide indicators of progress and warning signals of trouble. Thus in the earlier period statistics were mainly employed in the third of the uses described above—to map the course of events, to indicate what was wrong, but not to determine the extent of the action which should follow.

[1] See p. 113 below.　　　　　　　　　　　[2] [87].
[3] For example, the Census of Production (1907), the Cost of Living Index (1914), National Income Estimates (1941).

In any case, the rudimentary statistics of the last century could not have sustained heavier responsibilities. The recent growth of numerical knowledge has been stimulated by, and has in turn made possible, the development of 'planning', which sometimes means that the numerical extent of an action must be determined by solving the equations of some model. An example (in Chapter IX) is the determination of the size of budget surplus or deficit necessary to prevent serious inflation or deflation—a piece of 'planning' which became necessary when the convention of a balanced budget was abandoned. Another example, illuminating though somewhat negative, is in Chapter IV. It would have been within the compass of nineteenth-century statistics to show a need to build more houses—for example, by giving evidence of over-crowding. But a 'planned' housing policy means, presumably, that the Government has an idea of how many houses are needed (to bring the housing stock to some desired size, distribution and standard) and has a policy which will result in the building of these houses in a defined period. This would require information about family structure, income distribution, the demand function for house-room, and so on—information which is still not fully available in 1953.

There are many such gaps, and there is likely to be continued pressure to expand statistical knowledge so that they may be filled. At present this deliberate use of numerical facts in deciding policy is subject to a double weakness. A poor 'model' of reality may have been chosen—a wrong decision may have been made as to which interactions to allow for, and which to ignore. This weakness may be due either to a wrong judgement of the future, or to inadequate knowledge of the past. But even if a good model is chosen, it may yield false results because of uncertainties and errors in its statistical input. The combined effect of these weaknesses is that there are wide areas of economic policy or 'planning' where the use of statistics is theoretically conceivable but at present quite impossible. But decisions still have to be made: there must be a housing programme, even if we do not know how to regulate its size. If we cannot walk in the daylight of full knowledge, moonlight is still preferable to complete darkness—a doubtful figure may be much better than none at all.

The use of the word 'planning' may awaken echoes of controversy, but it need not here be associated with any particular economic theory or system. During the period which we are reviewing, there has un-doubtedly been a trend towards a more deliberate and scientific under-standing of the economy. This is seen quite clearly in the actions of firms in 'free-enterprise' economies, which increasingly rely on techniques such as market research and cost accountancy to give pre-cision to decisions which used to be made on the 'hunch' of a manager.

It is of course true that a highly 'controlled' economy, such as that of the U.S.S.R., requires an extensive statistical system; but so also does the work of the Council of Economic Advisers in the United States. Indeed, the statistical problems are likely to be more complex, and the attention they require more extensive, when 'planning' is attempted in a country with numerous decision units having much freedom of action.

THE 'OUTSIDE' USER OF STATISTICS

The discussion so far has concentrated on the needs of those who make decisions within the Government. But the private user of statistics, outside the ranks of Ministers and civil servants, is also exceedingly important; his work must not be regarded as a mere by-product. We can distinguish two classes of private user. One includes those who are interested in general policy—in recording what has happened, in assessing what is being done, in examining the possibilities and the implications of alternatives. The other consists largely of business men who require some particular selected statistics to throw light on the problems and prospects of their trade.

The 'general' users—applied economists, politicians out of office, historians and so on—begin at some disadvantage. They can hardly ever achieve the breadth of view, the direct access to up-to-date information, the knowledge of statistical difficulties which are possible to statisticians in the Government service. In some fields they will necessarily be excluded from detailed knowledge by the requirements of confidentiality. These disadvantages must not be increased by needless failure to publish statistics or make them available—or by failure to show how they have been obtained, and what errors they contain. The attitude that 'these are mysteries too high for the layman to understand' is refreshingly rare in British official life; but it is not entirely absent, and it would be a pity if it gained ground.

These assertions rest on a belief in the importance of discussion and criticism. If 'laymen' cannot criticize policy because they cannot get access to the facts, a dangerous power is given to the policy-makers. If there is no informed group, fully supplied with facts, which can be thinking freely about future changes in policy, the conduct of affairs will tend to become inflexible. In particular, political controversy will tend to be sterile if Her Majesty's Opposition is rendered incapable of planning intelligent alternative policies. Nor must we forget that those busy with current affairs need the help of those who try to see the 'broad sweep of history', and should in return give the economic historian access to material while its limitations can still be understood.

The 'business' user will require timely information about the general economic situation within which his business has to operate, but he will also need special and detailed information about (for example) stocks and prices of raw materials, wage rates in allied trades, imports and exports of his product, the family, class and income structure of particular groups of consumers, and so on. This appetite for detail may well go beyond what is needed for internal Government purposes, and it will then have to be considered whether the State has a duty to provide extra detail free as a public service, or perhaps to provide it against payment.[1] With the growth of market research, and the tendency of large modern firms to employ statistical analyses of their prospects, it must be expected that the demands of business users will grow.

Within both these classes of 'outside' user a distinction can be made between the expert and the non-expert. The former group includes (for instance) academic statisticians and those employed wholly on statistical work in industry. The latter includes directors and managers of companies, politicians, journalists, and others whose use of statistics is occasional but not continuous. The expert will be practised in the interpretation of figures, and careful to search out their precise meaning and limitations; often he will be able to establish direct contact with those primarily responsible for collecting the data. But the non-expert will tend to take statistics at their face value, and may easily draw erroneous conclusions from them. If this is to be prevented, then the obligation to publish data must be extended; figures must be presented in a way which enables their essentials to be grasped and their limitations to be appreciated quickly and easily.

The interests of those outside Government service are in part cared for by the Interdepartmental Committee on Social and Economic Research,[2] whose terms of reference are:

> 'To survey and advise upon research work in Government Departments, and in particular (a) to bring to the notice of Departments the potential value for research purposes of the material which they collect and to suggest new methods and areas of collection; (b) to advise on how there could be made available to research workers information gathered for their own purposes by the Departments which has potential value as material for research.'

But the emphasis here is on research (mainly in universities), and not on current use by business men and others. We have the impression that the mass of material, not of course wholly statistical, in the Government departments is so great that the Interdepartmental Committee is necessarily extremely slow-moving. We shall discuss below[3] whether

---

[1] This method is used if special analyses of trade returns are wanted.
[2] See pp. 4–5 above.   [3] P. 159.

other means may not be needed to make effective the public interest in a sound statistical system.

There are, of course, many non-Government producers of economic statistics, as well as non-Government users: for instance, the British Iron and Steel Federation, the British Bureau of Non-Ferrous Metal Statistics, the Chamber of Shipping, nationalized industries, and market research agencies. But (as the Reference Table at the end of this book shows) the important economic information is mostly collected by Government. In broad outline it is fair to think of economic statistics as being collected by the State for its own needs, and then made available for private users.

CONCLUSION

We have tried to show the complex ways in which numerical information may be brought to bear on policy, and have suggested some of the limitations on its use. We have also shown that users of varying interests are to be found within and without the Government service; so that a statistical system has to be judged in two ways—its adequacy to the policy needs of the present and the future, and its conformity to the varying requirements of the different users. Some of the implications of these criteria will be worked out in the next chapter.

Before leaving the subject of 'statistics and economic policy', however, it is well to remember that, if the various users need the help and co-operation of the statistician, so also does the statistician need the co-operation of the public. If that co-operation is withdrawn—if the cry of 'snoopers' is raised—the Government statistician may find his position weakened and his funds reduced. It is not therefore his duty only, but also his interest, to create an intelligent and informed public opinion in statistical matters. There appears to be some substance in the complaint that British business men are more reluctant to give information than their United States counterparts, and impose more restrictive conditions of secrecy. This is a failure of public relations, and the statistician needs to show (by presenting relevant material in an attractive way) that he has information to give as well as to demand—and to give, not just to his immediate masters, but to a wider public.

CHAPTER III

A SUMMARY OF PROBLEMS

What were we looking for in the case-studies which form Chapters IV–IX, and in our general investigations? First, we hoped to analyse the kind of statistical help which is, or can be, given to the policy-maker; that is to say, to identify which of the ways of employing statistics (enumerated in Chapter II) were relevant in a particular instance. Next, we looked again at these uses of statistics in relation to the users, actual or potential, and tried to decide whether their needs were well provided for. The difficulties and problems revealed at this stage were soon seen to fall into a few classes, so that we obtained a kind of check-list of problems needing examination. The final step was to check whether these problems had all been given proper consideration in the case under examination.

In the first stage, we often found that the relation between statistics and policy appeared the more tenuous, the more detailed the examination we were able to give to it. Concepts such as 'the housing shortage', 'the future demand for coal', 'exceptional unemployment in an area', which the layman might expect to be capable of expression in more or less definite numbers, prove on examination to be exceedingly nebulous. The role of *judgement* in interpreting the factual basis of policy appeared, as we progressed, increasingly important. There is some danger that the reader, following the same line of discovery, may be led too easily and quickly to one of two opposite conclusions: *either* that the modern development of economic statistics is largely eyewash, and that the pretensions of 'planners' and statisticians should be deflated; *or* that there is need for a great extension of statistical and econometric knowledge, in order to give substance to the concepts now so nebulous.

We hope that the reader will try to suspend judgement on these matters, and that this book will not be quoted either as an attack on the work of statisticians, or as a demand for their unqualified advancement. There is of course some truth in both conclusions—some gaps in knowledge which can and should be filled, some statistical façades which should be torn down. But it is necessary to keep tight hold of two common-sense ideas: partial knowledge (provided it is recognized to be partial) is better than none at all; and much knowledge is necessarily partial and incomplete. There is no going back to the statistical darkness of the past; but the future does not hold promise of perfect knowledge, the perfect mechanistic model of the economic system. There will always be the uncertainties, the occasions for general judgements, discussed on p. 10. It follows that ways of thinking must be adapted to the risks of an uncertain world, not to the determinacies of a certain one. Chapter v (on Coal) and Chapter ix both illustrate the need for thinking in terms of ranges of possibility, rather than of single 'best estimates'.

When, in the second stage, we came to consider the needs of various users, we often discovered that some statistics attract public attention, and are used as a basis for criticism and comment, perhaps even for policy determination, while relevant messages from other figures are ignored. Thus, Chapter v shows the undue attention given to the absolute level of coal stocks. We were thus led beyond the question of *availability* of statistics to various users to that of their *presentation*—to a discussion of whether this seemed likely to help or to hinder people in reaching sound conclusions. It will be noticed that many economic statistics are collected for administrative or 'operational' reasons, and then diverted to serve wider purposes; this is the case, for instance, with the Exchange Control data used for the Balance of Payments, with many of the coal statistics, and so forth. This means that policy decisions may use statistics which (having been adapted) are not exactly what is wanted; an example is the use made of Inland Revenue figures of salaries, wages, profits and depreciation, which are not good 'fits' to the corresponding economic concepts. We have therefore considered, not only *gaps* (that is, types of statistics wholly absent), but also the possibility of improving the *relevance* to policy of existing statistics.

Sometimes relevant figures are available, but come too late to be used, so that imperfect preliminary estimates have to take their place. This is true, for instance, of agricultural income figures (Chapter vii), and of many of the 'national income' data discussed in Chapter ix. The *timing* of information is thus an important matter to be considered: an accurate figure which comes too late is worth less than a doubtful but timely estimate. This leads straight to a discussion of the *use of sampling*, which is an important way of obtaining figures more quickly, and which seems relatively neglected in the United Kingdom.

Chapter ix illustrates, not only the construction of an economic 'model', but also the fact that the action which follows from its use is determined by small changes in large aggregates. It thus forcibly illustrates the need for some discussion of possible *errors*. Elsewhere, too, the need for indications of *reliability* (and explanations of revisions) comes to light; for instance, in Chapters vii and viii. This matter can also be considered as part of the problem of presentation: it is the duty of the statistician to tell those who use his figures about the snags and errors likely to occur in them. In fact, the user can hardly use them intelligently unless he is given a *description* of how they are obtained. We shall see that one of the weakest points in British statistics is the paucity of descriptions of method and discussions of reliability.

We do not discuss the *organization* of British statistical work until Chapter XII, but it must be remembered that the virtues and faults revealed in the chapters preceding it are the virtues and faults of a particular statistical system, organized in a way not always followed in other countries. Possibly the system might be improved; possibly it needs to be more conscious of efficiency—that is, of obtaining a balance of effort and results in its various parts. We have not thought it helpful to give long lists of extra information which might, in an ideal world, be collected and made available. The plain fact is that, for some years to come, it will be difficult to find the money and the skilled manpower to maintain the existing array of British economic statistics. It is all the more important, therefore, to deploy resources skilfully and without waste; and the problems summarized in this chapter should, as they are revealed, be discussed within this framework of the skilful use of limited statistical resources.

CHAPTER IV

HOUSING

In 1951 the value of new housing built in the United Kingdom was some £335 million, 18 % of gross fixed capital formation[1] in that year. The number of houses demolished or falling out of use during the year is unknown; but a large proportion of the 201,856 permanent houses completed were probably net additions to the nation's stock of houses, comprising some 13½ million 'structurally separate dwellings'. Net capital formation—that is, the *addition* to the capital stock—is not officially estimated, because of the difficulty of assessing what is required to maintain capital intact; but even after allowing an offset for the under-maintenance of existing houses, it is clear that a quarter to a third of net capital formation must be in the form of housing.

This is a substantial part of the nation's investment programme. How is it determined? What facts can help to decide whether it is 'better' to build 300,000 or 200,000 houses a year? We shall start by inquiring whether the existing statistics enable us to assess the size of the housing shortage, or the capacity of the building industry to build new houses. We shall find that they do not; the function of statistics in this field of policy is to provide background information, helpful but incomplete, and to throw some light on the implications of possible changes, or the results of changes which have been made. But even if we cannot build a model which can show just how many houses should be built this year, it may still be worth while to improve the existing statistics, so that they answer more directly and accurately the questions which the policy-maker would like to put; we shall find some examples of such improvements in the course of our survey.

First we must describe some of the background. Most of the houses built in post-war years have been built for or by local authorities, or other public bodies, for letting. But at the end of 1951 there were still four local authorities in England and Wales who had completed no houses of their own since the war; on the other hand, rates of completion double the national average can be found. Some authorities had permitted no 'private-enterprise' building, others had allowed it to the full extent permitted by Government regulation. Broadly speaking, the 'typical' post-war house in England and Wales has been a local authority house for letting, attracting a subsidy both from the central government and from the rates. This house is not rent-controlled, but

---

[1] On the new definition, used in Table 33 of [34c].

it has commonly been let at between a half and two-thirds of the rent at which it would be an economic proposition to an unsubsidized private landlord. On the other hand, it has had to compete in public estimation with rent-controlled houses, perhaps with fewer amenities, but at rents as low as a half of the subsidized rent of the post-war house of comparable size. The local authority houses have usually been built by private builders, only 8 % of the labour force being directly employed by the authorities; but the heading 'private builders' in the *Housing Returns* refers, somewhat confusingly, to houses built, under licence, for private purchasers. These houses, about 15 % of the total in 1952, have mostly been built for owner-occupation; they have been limited in size, like the local authority houses, and there have been restrictions designed to prevent their resale at a profit.

In Scotland practically all post-war housing has been built, to let, by local authorities and the Scottish Special Housing Association. In recognition of the greater housing needs of Scotland, and the special difficulties of securing an adequate rate of building, a higher subsidy has been payable. In Northern Ireland, where there is also a considerable leeway in housing to be made up, subsidies at roughly the Scottish level have been paid, but an entirely different policy has been followed. Private-enterprise building, both for sale and for letting, has been allowed, and has attracted a capital subsidy for houses up to the size of a normal English council house. Nearly half the 'public authority' building has been undertaken by the Northern Ireland Housing Trust, so that the role of individual local authorities has been much more limited than in Great Britain. Northern Ireland is also unique in having carried out a modest reform of rent restriction.

HOW MANY HOUSES ARE NEEDED?

The result of these varied interventions in the housing market is that it is difficult to attach any meaning to the 'demand', or even to the 'need', for houses. The demand for houses to let, with benefit of subsidy, is almost everywhere greater than the supply; this is the 'housing shortage' which shows itself in long local authority waiting lists. But this demand is inflated in two ways. First, the protection given under rent restriction means that small families who live in large rent-restricted houses have an incentive to stay there, and not much incentive to have others to live with them. The proportion of small households has grown in the last twenty years; since they are relatively spaciously housed, the average number of rooms per person has risen. Secondly, the 'council house', though it may seem expensive in relation to an older house, is new and often pleasantly situated and spaciously planned, and it carries a large subsidy which is not (like a food subsidy) universal, but goes to the people who are lucky enough to be allotted a post-war house—a privileged class of one in fifteen, subsidized by the general body of tax-payers. There is nothing to be lost, and may be much to be gained by having one's name on a local authority waiting list—or on two or three, if one can overcome the rather sketchy safeguards against duplication. Indeed, the lists would be much longer if some people did not consider that (because they have no children, or because they have a high wage) they would not 'stand a chance' of being allocated a house, and thus need not apply.

The sum of the numbers on all waiting lists is thus no direct help in deciding how many houses should be built. It may be too large, because (despite occasional reviews) it contains substantial duplication, and many applications from people who have since housed themselves privately; on the other hand, this may be offset by its failure to include people who would gladly take a house of the size and rent of the post-war local authority house, but cannot prove 'need' on the standard locally being applied, and the complementary failure to include people who could prove 'need', but could not pay the rent asked. The waiting lists tend, in fact, to relate to medium and large families with medium family incomes; the needs of others are to some extent met by the houses vacated by those moving into new dwellings.

Nevertheless, the trend of the total on waiting lists would be an interesting indicator, and it would be useful if it were published. It would also be illuminating to know how the benefits and hardships of present policy are distributed. What are the incomes, families and ages of the people allocated new houses, and of people living in rent-restricted property? What is the net effect of rent restriction and the high demand for houses on the economic position of landlords? How many empty and under-used houses are there, and how many are falling out of use through disrepair? We know very little about the answers to any of these questions, and, in the absence of this knowledge, we cannot adequately judge the effectiveness of present housing policy. As we shall see below, there is a strong case for a properly designed national sample survey of housing facts and needs, and the larger local authorities might well obtain and publish such information for their own areas.

The higher prices, and keen demands, for second-hand and older houses for sale give little help in deciding what should be done. These prices have reflected the limitations on building for owner-occupation, especially (in Great Britain) the size limitation: and the drying-up of the supply and turnover of houses to let by private landlords, because of the fixed rents and great security of tenure under rent restriction. They give no indication of the numbers who genuinely wish to build for owner-occupation at full current building prices—either with or without the counter-attraction of a possible rent-restricted tenancy. Nor do they tell us how many houses would be built for private letting if rents were free. The experience of Northern Ireland, where the speculative builder has to sell his subsidized house by high-pressure advertising, suggests that the demand for houses for sale might be quite quickly exhausted.

But again we must remember that partial information is better than none at all. Facts about the trend of house prices in selected areas, and about the turnover of houses sold, would be useful. A little information on prices is available privately from building societies, but more is needed, and it might be obtained in the course of a national housing survey.

Can we proceed from another angle, and consider the physical 'need' for houses, leaving the difficult economic problem of paying for them for separate and later consideration? This might seem relatively simple. The physical need for a commodity like butter is difficult to define; in one sense it is zero, because a physiologically acceptable substitute, margarine, exists. The effect of subsidizing butter is to increase demand for an expensive source of fats, mostly imported, without necessarily improving nutrition at all. But there is no substitute for house-room; there is a presumption that family life is more stable, a better background for children, and more pleasant if dwellings do not have to be shared; and a possible[1] first target, therefore, is to have a house for each family, with a small excess in all areas to allow easy mobility. (The 'need' for housing would be greater than this, because there is a large amount of bad property which needs to be cleared and rebuilt.) Have we statistics which would enable us to estimate the surplus of families over dwellings?

According to the sample returns from the 1951 Census of Population,[2] there were 13·3 million 'structurally separate dwellings' and 14·5 million 'households' in that year in Great Britain. 2·1 million households were sharing dwellings, the number of shared dwellings being 0·9 million. There was thus an apparent deficit of 1·2 million dwellings. But these statistics—the principal source of information on the subject—require interpretation. A 'household' consists of a group of people 'boarding' together, and may thus include lodgers receiving board as well as lodging, grown-up children, married couples living with their parents as a single family—any of whom might wish, if more houses were available, to set up as separate households. In other words, the

---

[1] Possible, but not obvious; there is evidence that in some areas much sharing of homes would continue even if there were empty houses—partly for convenience and partly for economy.

[2] [53].

number of households is not independent of the number of dwellings. The households can, however, be divided into 12½ million 'primary family unit' households and two million 'composite' households. A 'primary family unit' household is a single person, or a family which has no relations living with it other than parents and grandparents, unmarried brothers and sisters, or childless widowed brothers and sisters, of the man and wife. The composite households include others—typically, married children. These composite households are found to contain about one million 'family nuclei'—that is, married couples, or lone parents with children. If these were all separately housed, the total requirement would be 15½ million houses. But even this figure is not quite what we want; many of the 'family nuclei' would prefer to live with relations, while many grandparents might like to have a place of their own.[1]

Furthermore, a 'structurally separate dwelling' is a house, flat or maisonette either built as a separate dwelling or obtained, through the dividing up of a house, as an entirely separate and private part. A man who rents three rooms in a house does not occupy a 'structurally separate dwelling' unless the three rooms are behind a single front door, giving access to the street or to a common stair or landing to which the public has access. There are clearly great numbers of houses which are divided so as to give adequate privacy to two or more families, but which would be regarded as single dwellings for the purposes of this definition. Finally, just as some non-householders would like a separate dwelling, so some who rank as householders may prefer to share; an aged parent may rank as a separate householder, by virtue of cooking on his or her own gas ring, but may not need or wish to have a separate 'house'.[2]

These figures, therefore, like the other indicators we have discussed, confirm the impression that we need a larger absolute number of dwellings, but give only a vague idea of the size of the deficiency. If we now allow economic considerations in at the back door, the situation becomes vaguer still; for there are certainly some families which would prefer cheap shared accommodation to expensive privacy. Nor can we get much help by considering how many households are overcrowded. The 1951 Census shows that some 283,000 households in Great Britain were living more than two persons to a (principal) room, of which almost half were in Scotland, and about a fifth were composite households; but since the average for all households is only about three-quarters of a person per room, this is a problem of the maldistribution of housing accommodation (which is aggravated by rent restriction) rather than of

---

[1] For further details (including numbers of rooms occupied) see [53], pp. 182 et seq.

[2] For the difficulties of other methods of estimating the 'need' for houses, and the number of houses between censuses, see Marian Bowley, in Kendall [102].

its absolute shortage. There may be an absolute deficiency of houses suitable in size and rent for large families with low incomes, but the numbers concerned are small.

Slightly more solid ground can be reached by considering the number of families who, by direct investigation, appear to be badly or inadequately housed. It is difficult to know what standard should be applied. Just as some people voluntarily choose to live on a diet below the physiological optimum, in order to have more money to spend on other things, so some may rightly choose to live in old-fashioned, or ugly, houses whose cheapness compensates for their lack of amenities. There are clearly some houses which are in an advanced stage of decay, which are in some cases a danger to the health and safety of the occupants, and which are considered not worth 'patching up'—though this is a judgement difficult to make when the economic costs of housing are as obscure as they are at present. The under-maintenance which is a natural consequence of rent-restriction will tend to produce a steady flow of houses into this class of the irredeemably decayed. Seebohm Rowntree's latest survey of York[1] shows, on four possible definitions, practically no overcrowding among working-class families. On the other hand, Rowntree found 22·9 % of working-class families sharing a house— a deficiency of some 4,000 houses—and he notes that 'save in a few cases the sharing of a house is not due to financial stringency, but to the inability of one of the families to obtain a house of their own' (p. 89). There were about 1,000 families with lodgers. Out of about 30,000 houses in York (18,000 occupied by working-class families) the City Council had made provision, under the Town and Country Planning Act, 1947, for the demolition of some 6,000 over a period of twenty years. 1,659 houses were scheduled to be dealt with in the first five years of this period, this including 'all the houses in York that can for any reason (such as the decay of the structure, or the absence of water laid on in the house) be described as slum properties' (p. 82). It is interesting to note that, in his corresponding survey fifty years before,[2] Rowntree found practically no sharing of houses, but substantial overcrowding; he placed about a fifth of the houses of the city in Class 3, slums or near-slums even according to the standards of the time.

This kind of direct survey can thus give, for an area, some indication of the absolute deficiency of houses, of the need to abate overcrowding, and of the immediate needs of slum clearance. As the Development Plans made under the Town and Country Planning Act are brought together and analysed, they will give some indication of a total need for housing, though very different criteria will probably have been applied

[1] B. Seebohm Rowntree and G. R. Lavers [115].
[2] B. Seebohm Rowntree [114].

in different areas.[1] This lack of uniformity will make it difficult to judge the relative needs of different areas. Nor do any of the statistics we have mentioned earlier help. A comparison of waiting lists is no use when they are drawn up on different principles. A comparison of numbers of households and dwelling units, which (as we have seen) is not very helpful for the country as a whole, is even less so for local areas, in which the number of households will be mainly determined by the number of dwellings in the area. In local areas, too, the problem of judging the future growth or decline of a community will be a difficult one.

This survey of the possible ways of assessing the 'demand' or 'need' for houses is a discouraging one. Normal criteria of profitability do not apply in an area so much subject to intervention on grounds of social policy; the State is not satisfied that houses should be built simply until it ceases to be profitable to build more. But no other satisfactory guide is available. As far as we can judge, housing policy since the war has assumed that the deficiency of houses, together with the number which ought at once to be demolished, comes to so great a sum that the 'need' can be considered to be boundless, and the problem reduced to one of allocating a block of resources to housing and making the fullest possible use of it. The limitations have been entirely on the supply side, which we will next discuss. But this easy assumption cannot stand for ever. What more can be done to establish the relevant facts?

One possible answer is that, since housing is a local matter, the 'need' for it can only appear as the sum total of the very various ideas of local Councils—the adding up of figures from a heterogeneous mass of Development Plans. We would welcome more publication of facts and figures by local authorities—Birmingham sets a distinguished example; but there is a national policy to be decided, and some better background of national statistics seems to be needed. Three things are wanted. The first is more information, however vague, about *trends*—for example in waiting lists, turnover of houses, vacancies, and house prices. Some of this information exists in the Departments, but more should be published. The second need is for the social data required for the assessment of rent and subsidy policy—who benefits and who suffers hardship. The third need is for more information about what people want; at defined rent levels how many potential households exist? It is true that the answer to this will ultimately appear if enough houses are built to saturate the demand, but in the meantime a few more rough indications would be helpful. The second and third needs could be met to some extent by a nationally planned sample survey; and this could also establish how many existing houses fall below some nationally defined level of tolerability, and thus need replacement.

[1] Bowley in [102], p. 308.

HOW MANY HOUSES CAN BE SUPPLIED?

If it is supposed that there is an immediate housing need large in proportion to present annual rates of building, what are the limits which restrict the speed of building? Have we the facts which would enable us to estimate a possible speed of building for a year, or for five years, ahead?

In a particular area, the shortage of building sites may be a decisive limitation; but this is not very relevant for the country as a whole. The other limitations—all of which have applied since the war, at different times or places—are the shortage of labour (especially of particular grades of labour, such as bricklayers and plasterers); shortages of materials; and inability to finance an adequate volume of imported materials.[1] The latter can be disposed of first. The import content of an average house in 1951 was of the order of £200, the greater part of which was accounted for by the use of $1\frac{1}{2}$ standards of timber, while much of the rest was lead, copper and brass. At this time, severe restrictions on the use of timber had already been enforced, and economy will be easily maintained while timber remains at a high price. The use of foreign exchange can be reduced by lowering standards and sizes; it remains sufficiently large to be a likely subject of restriction when there are balance-of-payments difficulties. We can see no statistical ground on which it is possible to determine that house-building should be a privileged claimant on foreign-exchange resources. It is possible to argue that industrial efficiency would be increased by greater mobility of labour, and that this would be facilitated by a larger flow of new houses; but even if the argument is true, it is impossible to put a numerical value on it.

The annual return by contractors, required in Great Britain under Defence Regulation 56 AB, obtains information about the number of 'male operatives and apprentices' and 'working principals' by ten trade divisions, and the number and inflow of apprentices by nine divisions. It also asks for a return (divided by regions of the country) of the number of male operatives and apprentices employed on site preparation and erection of permanent houses and flats, on other housing work (that is, repair, maintenance, conversion and adaptation), and on corresponding divisions of non-housing work. The 'site return' from individual building sites (monthly), and the quarterly contractor's return both ask for total numbers of men employed. There is thus available to the Ministry of Works an annual return of labour employed in the

---

[1] There is, of course, also the general shortage of 'savings'; this means that investment as a whole must be restricted, but it is possible (as the experience of 1952 has shown) to restrict something other than housing.

building and civil engineering industry, by trades, and an annual return and monthly estimate of labour employed on housing. There is *not* any direct way of dividing the housing labour by trades, though an indirect estimate can be made by considering the number of man-hours of different kinds of labour required in an average house. The Ministry of Labour has, of course, information about vacancies of various kinds in the building trades.

Now new housing is less than a quarter, by value, of the total building and civil engineering output, and it employs less than a fifth of the man-power which produces that output. In the building and civil engineering industries, new housing work competes for manpower with a larger amount of other work employing the same tradesmen, such as the building of shops, schools and hospitals and the repair and adaptation of houses. The statistics, therefore, though they may give warning of a general shortage in a particular trade (for example plasterers), cannot indicate whether this shortage is a decisive limitation on housing output; for this depends on the relative priorities given to different kinds of building work. The total output of the industry probably depends not so much on its total labour force as on the size of the core of skilled men. Since their skills are for the most part specific to the industry, and their numbers only change slowly as old men retire and apprentices are trained, the total output should be able to be estimated for a little time ahead; but the output of a particular section such as new housing depends on a political decision on priorities for which we can offer no statistical basis. What statistics can do, however, is to display the *implications* of a decision—given the trends of manpower, so much more housing means so much less elsewhere; and this is an important function.

Within the limits of a fixed skilled labour force, an increase in output could be obtained by a rise in productivity. In 1947, output per man-hour in house-building in England and Wales was about 31 % down on pre-war; in 1949 and 1951 the figure was 20 %. These estimates were obtained by the Committee on the Cost of House-Building,[1] which was set up in 1947 and released in 1952, having first reported that estimates of cost could and should continue to be published by the Ministry of Housing and Local Government. We consider it important that studies of productivity in house-building should continue, for experience over a longer time may make it possible to eliminate some of the possible causes of this decline, and to assess the relative importance of others. The causes appear to be deep-seated and not removable by any simple act of policy.

The conclusion so far is that, on the side of manpower, the statistics may give warning of possible shortages affecting the industry as a whole;

[1] England and Wales: see Girdwood [61]. There was a separate Committee for Scotland.

but that the extent to which these shortages affect house-building in particular depends on whether this branch of building work is given priority over (say) factories, schools, or repair work. The 'overloading' of the industry, which has frequently been quoted as a cause of low productivity, arises from a failure to determine and enforce priorities. The choice between houses and schools has to be made quite outside any market, and without the benefit of any statistical foundation for determining relative priorities.

Exactly the same applies in the case of materials. At various times, bricks, timber, electrical goods, special castings, lead, copper pipe and many other things have been in short supply. Statistical information about building materials is available in fair volume—some published, and much more in the Ministry of Works' internal statistical digest. But for many materials new housing is not the dominant consumer, so that once again any shortage is not an absolute limitation on housing construction. Some components (such as baths or gas cookers) are mainly needed for new houses, but their output can usually be stepped up, for example by diverting iron-casting production from other uses. A true limitation on the side of supply would arise from a scarcity of a material produced solely for the building industry, and mainly for new houses. Bricks are a fair example of this; and the investment planner would certainly need to keep an eye on the manpower and stock position in the brick industry.

It is possible that the supply of factors of production may set a lower as well as an upper bound to output. It may be argued, for instance, that much building manpower is unlikely to find employment elsewhere; that various attempts to reduce the numbers employed in the industry have been fruitless, the labour released disappearing into minor repair work rather than into other industries. It is certainly true that the total number employed in the industry has remained remarkably steady for more than five years. If any meaning can be given to output per head in real terms in the whole industry, the task of the investment planner would appear simple; he has to make some assumption about productivity in the coming period, and arrange the programme of work so as to give full employment to the constant total of manpower.

This, however, is of little use in solving the problem we are discussing here; the problem of allocation between different forms of building would remain. In any case, it would be singularly defeatist to suppose that (arguing from the experience of a few exceptional years of buoyant employment) the manpower of the building industry is for ever constant.

THE PROBLEM OF PRIORITIES

If the process to be described in Chapter ix yields a grand total, the value of gross investment likely to be possible in a coming year, can we determine the proper level of housing activity by considering, first the division between building and non-building investment, and then the division between different kinds of building work? As we have seen, the price mechanism will be of little use in making this decision—partly because it has been so much interfered with, by rent restriction and subsidies, and partly because much building work (for example hospitals, schools, road works) is of a kind whose 'value' cannot readily be assessed. It may be that, if rent restriction were abolished and rents allowed to find their own level, they would still be below the economic rents of comparable new houses, so that the demand for new houses would be small; but this is only conjecture.

In the absence of a pricing system, one can only fall back on some general indications of priority. For instance, the maintenance and repair of capital assets which are not obsolete may be more important than the creation of new assets. Where a machine must necessarily be housed in a building, that building acquires a place on the scale of importance determined by what it contains. A house similarly may acquire a direct value as a factor of production if it is built to house a 'key worker'; hence the tied cottage, the importance of building houses in mining areas, and so on. The State being committed to the principle of supplying education to all children, a new school may have a first call on building resources if otherwise children would go without schooling.

But these indications do not take us very far. The plain fact is that there are no rules for deciding the economic value of most 'social' investment; and there are no statistics which would enable us to decide how much more would be produced, now or in the future, if people were to a defined extent better housed,[1] educated in finer school buildings, or nursed in more spacious hospitals. Since houses last for a very long time, house-building can be at a low level for a number of years without seriously affecting the stock of houses; and a stern economist, observing that there is enough house-room to avoid overcrowding, might argue that in a time of economic stress, when quick returns are needed, new housing has a very low importance. The fact that this

[1] No doubt labour mobility is less during a housing shortage, but the weight to be given to this is quite uncertain. We know very little about movements of labour between industries (a statistical gap which ought to be filled); but a great many men can change their job without changing their residence, and the number of changes of residence taking place each year is very large. There is some evidence on this in Newton and Jeffery [67], but more knowledge of internal migration would be valuable.

argument is not generally accepted in Britain at the present time shows
the importance which people give to better housing as an immediately
desirable good; public opinion polls have often shown 'housing' as one
of the chief problems on which Government action is hoped for.

CONCLUSION

At the end of this long search for assistance in deciding the size of a
housing programme, therefore, we seem to be left with little more than
the fact that the electorate would like to have more houses. The elector
is offered a chance of a specific material benefit at a managed price,
carrying with it a liability to heavier taxation which is merged in the
rates and the general tax burden; he is not making up his mind about
the economic merits of the case. Although the various statistics we have
discussed all have their uses in planning or in carrying out a housing
programme, they prove to give us no answer to our original question:
How large should that programme be?

It was important to establish this, because it is easy to expect too
much of statistics. In the terminology of Chapter II, we have here no
general 'model' of the housing market. What we have got is a set of
partial relations, with the aid of which statistics can help to suggest the
implications of possible lines of policy, or the repercussions of what is
actually happening in one part of the building industry on the rest of
the industry and the economy. But we have seen that a good many of
the indicators which one would like to have, to perform this important
function, are missing or imperfect; much more knowledge is wanted
about trends, and about the stock of houses and how it is used. We have
made some suggestions for improvement, but a more careful examination is needed. The presentation of existing statistics, for example in the
Housing Returns, leaves much to be desired; and the division between the
Ministries of Works and Housing cuts awkwardly across the field. We
suggest that the Departments concerned with building should organize
a joint inquiry, with a view to extending and improving their statistical
material.

CHAPTER V

COAL

Although from a very long-term point of view there is a certain element of artificiality in considering only one part, even if it is of major importance, of the fuel and power industry as a whole,[1] such a course is a perfectly reasonable one from a medium or short-term standpoint. Indeed, any attempt to discuss the fuel and power problem from a statistical angle as a coherent whole would probably end by examining each of the main sources of supply singly and in turn.

In this chapter the following mode of treatment will be adopted. First, the sources of information about the coal industry available to those inside and outside the industry and the civil service will be discussed. Secondly, we shall consider how this information can be used to assist in the making of policy decisions or programmes for a period of six months or a year ahead. Thirdly, our sights will be raised somewhat so that the adequacy of existing knowledge and of its present method of analysis in helping in the formation of longer term policies for the coal industry may be assessed.

THE AVAILABLE STATISTICS

A detailed account of the 'Statistics relating to the Coal Industry' has been provided[2] by Mr R. F. George, who is head of the very large statistical section of the National Coal Board. It is not our purpose to duplicate the work so ably done by Mr George; attention will merely be drawn in the broadest terms to the information made available from time to time. It is desirable, however, to remember the four main classes into which Mr George divides coal-mining statistics, that is, output, manpower, effort and earnings. For the present purpose a fifth class relating to distribution, the statistics of which are the responsibility of the Ministry of Fuel and Power and not of the Coal Board, may be added.

Few, if any, industries provide the public with as much statistical information as does the coal industry. Although coal statistics have maintained their leading position for a great many years, nevertheless the fuel difficulties of the Second World War caused a further elaboration of the statistical service, especially with respect to coal consumption.

[1] See 'The European Coal Problem' in *Economic Survey of Europe, 1951* [80].
[2] George in Kendall [102], p. 87.

At present there is a weekly press statement by the Ministry of Fuel and Power giving the latest details of output, employment and productivity in the coal industry and of coal consumption and stocks. The Coal Board's *Annual Report*, complete with its financial accounts and comprehensive statistical tables, is published about midsummer each year. There is also a *Quarterly Statistical Statement of the Costs of Production, Proceeds and Profits of Collieries* which has now been published for thirty years. Every year with some delay the Ministry of Fuel and Power produces its annual *Statistical Digest*, which includes, as well as statistics relating to the coal industry, information concerning electricity, gas, coke, manufactured fuel, benzole and tar, and petroleum. This digest, while publishing in greater detail many figures available elsewhere, provides the sole source of published information about the equipment of the coal industry. It is a very comprehensive publication, and its value is increased by the introductions to the sections, which explain in a clear way the historical background and definitions of the figures.

Those occupying official positions within the industry can gain access to even more sources of knowledge. The Coal Board's Finance Department, for example, computes very detailed costings and shows especial interest in output from Saturday working, since this coal is much more costly from the Board's point of view than the output resulting from normal hours of work. In the Ministry of Fuel and Power a number of returns are compiled for internal purposes only. Some of these relate to particular items of temporary importance while others are summary statements drawn up periodically. Thus, in addition to the weekly press statement, a weekly confidential statement on solid fuels is compiled in the Ministry. In this statement, all the key figures for the current period are compared with the corresponding details for the corresponding period a year ago and with the expected figures derived from the Ministry's 'budget'.

All the figures given in the different published sources are, almost without exception, used for administrative purposes at some level or other in the coal industry's hierarchy. They can therefore be regarded as being reasonably reliable; for where statistics are used for practical purposes at a level other than that of policy-making, this usually ensures a fair level of respectability. The only major field where such a check has in the past been incomplete is the Census of Production return for the coal industry.

In all big undertakings it is often difficult to ensure a reasonably consistent interpretation of statistical definitions. In the nationalized coal industry the Divisional Statistical Officers are simultaneously responsible both to their local headquarters and to the statistical section at the National Coal Board itself, and this is intended to prevent serious discrepancies from arising. But even so absolute uniformity cannot be expected, and in general it is safer to rely on inter-temporal rather than on inter-spatial comparisons; this is especially true so far as the movements of workers are concerned. Although there are about 500 (out of a total of about 1,400) mines not owned by the Coal Board and operating under licence, their statistical eccentricities, if they have any, would not have serious results since these mines account for only about 1 % of the manpower of the industry and for a similar proportion of its total output.

If there are any deficiencies to be found in the width of coverage or the depth of the coal industry's statistics, they exist in those dealing with the labour force itself; though in general the labour statistics are much better than for other industries. The deficiencies are not, perhaps, surprising in an industry in which industrial relations were until recently far from satisfactory. There is a dearth of knowledge both about the character of the labour force itself and about certain aspects of the rewards that it receives. Thus while the movements of labour in and out of the industry are recorded by divisions and by age, it is impossible to discover whether or not a large proportion of those who leave the industry do so after a comparatively short stay.[1] A significant part of the miner's reward is received in kind, that is in the form of free or concessionary coal, clothing, lamps and house-room. The precise variation in these emoluments from pit to pit appears to be difficult to trace.

Although the public is presented with a large amount of numerical information about the coal industry, not enough help is given in the intelligent interpretation of the available figures. Some attention might well be given to presenting the more important details with a com-mentary, which would draw attention to the human and technical factors involved of which the layman is not generally aware.

STATISTICS AND SHORT-TERM PROGRAMMES

Coal, like housing, has a managed price, and there is very little of the free play of market forces in deciding output or selling policy. An effort is therefore made to balance supply and demand by drawing up a 'coal budget' every six months or year, and trying to influence its constituent items so that it is consistent. This must be done without pushing forward too many problems to the next period—for example without drawing down stocks to an 'unsafe' level.

[1] In 1952 there was at least a suspicion that in Lancashire some men entered the training centres in the hope that the textile industry would recover from its recession by the time that their training as miners was completed.

The problems which must be faced will be illuminated, but not solved, by drawing up the first trial 'coal budget' for the appropriate period. It is most unlikely that both sides of such a budget will be in balance, but the statistical exercise should make clear the various ways by which it is possible to achieve some sort of equilibrium. When a decision, which must inevitably be based on judgement, has been taken about the measure or measures necessary to balance the coal budget, the amended and balanced budget can be used as a convenient means of recording the decisions of the Coal Board and the Government. A potential coal deficiency may be circumvented by reducing coal allocations to industry or domestic consumers or both, by reducing exports, by increasing imports, or conceivably by raising coal prices,[1] or by a combination of any number of these actions.

The compilation of a coal budget requires the making of forecasts of the total demand and the total supply of coal during the period in question. Although the balanced coal budget is normally presented in terms of the total amount of coal to be mined or to be consumed in six months, say, the actual taking of decisions, or indeed any *ex post* examination of their justification, needs to be based on forecasts of how both demand and supply are likely to be *changing* throughout the period: for example, *x* million tons of coal are likely to be mined in total, but the *rate* of output will probably rise over the period from an annual rate of *y* million tons to one of *z* million tons. Obviously a balance between a rising output and a rising consumption is not at all the same thing as a fortuitous equality, in a particular period, between a falling output and a rising consumption. Rates of change are, in many fields, the most important statistics.

The supplies of coal are derived from deep mines, opencast workings and imports. Of these, imports, because of the expense involved, are to be regarded as an exceptional balancing measure provided always that there is sufficient time to give the necessary orders before the period arrives to which the budget applies. If, however, time is short the forecast of imports must be based on the likely deliveries in discharge of orders already given. Opencast coal output can be forecast without undue difficulty.

As we have seen, there exists a wealth of statistical information about the supplies of deep-mined coal that have been forthcoming in the past. Other things being equal (an important qualification), the output of deep-mined coal in any period is dependent on the total manpower in

---

[1] Such a course is rather unlikely to be adopted on its own when demand for coal is already artificially restricted, since the amount by which prices must be raised in order to secure any further reduction in demand would be somewhat hazardous to estimate. Rises in prices will, however, increase the effectiveness of any existing direct controls on consumption.

the industry and on its distribution—that is, at the face, elsewhere under-ground, and on the surface. The attendance of the labour force is of great importance, and forecasts must be made of the shifts likely to be lost by absenteeism, voluntary or involuntary, by disputes, and by mishaps of various kinds. Output will also depend on the level of output per man-shift—that is, productivity—which in turn will be affected in part by the recent deployment of new capital equipment and by other improvements in the mines.

The necessary projections or forecasts of coal output can either be based on an analysis of the apparent trends in the global figures of man-power, attendance and productivity, coupled with an estimate of the effects of any new factor likely to be operating in the future, or they can be built up by the Production Department of the National Coal Board after consultation with the management of the collieries under its control. In practice both methods are used to check and to reinforce one another. Individual mine managers may possibly base their own forecasts on assumptions which, though plausible on purely local con-siderations, are seen to be improbable or inconsistent when viewed from the point of view of the industry as a whole. For instance, so far as labour movements are concerned, the Manpower Department of the Board can draw on the advice and knowledge of the regional inspectors of the Ministry of Labour; such a source of information is not readily accessible at lower managerial levels. On the other hand, the colliery managers can often assess more accurately the effects of changes in local conditions than can the Production Department or the Statistical Section.[1]

For many of the factors, such as productivity, absenteeism, and labour movement, which influence the level of coal output in a period, indices of seasonal variation have been calculated after analysis of the statistics of past performance. Thus projected output for a period can be allocated to individual weeks, with appropriate allowances for the incidence of, say, holidays, and within the Coal Board itself[2] the correspondence between prognostication and actual performance can be watched.

It has been estimated that before the war a 1 % increase in the stock of capital employed in the coal industry—a tricky thing to define—was associated, other things being equal, with an increase in output of about $\frac{1}{4}$ %.[3] This result, which was based on an analysis of time series, appears to be consistent with a further unpublished investigation, of which the authors were told, based on cross-section data for the years 1946–50. It is of course a bold step to jump from 'association' to 'causality', and even if the rise in output could be attributed to an

---

[1] The Statistical Section is part of the Secretary's Department at the National Coal Board.
[2] These detailed forecasts are not published.
[3] See K. S. Lomax, 'Coal Production Functions for Great Britain' [105].

increase in the stock of capital as a cause, the results would shed no light on the short-term effects on productivity of an increase in plant and equipment.

For forecasting the inland consumption of coal, there is also plenty of historical information which can be used. Regression analysis has been employed in order to investigate the average relationship between the industrial consumption of various kinds of fuel and the level of industrial output, the weather and other factors. The forecasts actually inserted in the coal budget are based on the assumption of 'normal' weather conditions.

The requirements of coal for exports and bunkers must in part be a forecast—this applies to at least a proportion of coal bunkers—in part an estimate of inescapable obligations, and for the rest an item on which a policy decision must be taken in the process of balancing the budget.

THE ROLE OF STOCKS

At this point it will be useful to give special attention to the role of stocks in the problem of coal programming. Let us suppose, in order to simplify the situation, that all coal is consumed at home and that there is no possibility of importing coal. Further let us imagine for the moment that forecasts of both the demand and supply of coal lead to the conclusion that they are likely to be in equilibrium not only over the period concerned considered as a single block of time but also at each moment of time within it. Or in other words, the trend of the demand and the supply of coal are the same throughout the period.

As the events of the period for which forecasts have been prepared unfold themselves, not only will output and consumption differ from these forecasts according to the degree to which the basic assumptions are falsified by the departure of weather conditions from 'normality'[1] and by unanticipated changes in the level of industrial output, in the flow of labour into the coal industry, and so on, but there will be random fluctuations from week to week. If, therefore, the conversion of coal into heat and power is to proceed smoothly, a sufficient stock of coal must be held at the beginning of the period to give a *reasonable* assurance that neither the error inevitably inherent in forecasting nor random variations (of weather, output, etc.) will cause dislocation of industrial production or undue discomfort to domestic consumers. Even under the simplified and very favourable assumptions that we have so far made, the level of stocks required to *guarantee* immunity from trouble under the most unfavourable circumstances possible would be extremely high.

---

[1] A variation of 1° F. in the average annual temperature tends to alter annual consumption by 1½ million tons, other things being equal.

The holding of large stocks of coal would be very difficult and costly. Coal is bulky, and the storage capacity of both industrial and other consumers and of the collieries themselves is limited. Industry might have to increase its advances from the banks in order to finance such stocks, and the mere cost of dumping coal on the ground and lifting it again later would probably be from 5s. to 7s. a ton at 1952 prices. The rebuilding of such stocks, should they have been seriously depleted, would inevitably cause discomfort and dislocation to industrial production, since under the assumption which we have made it could only be achieved by cutting supplies to consumers. Thus the desirable *level* of stocks must be judged by balancing the risks of extremely adverse circumstances against the costs of holding these stocks. The *rate* at which stocks are built up or rebuilt to the desired level must be decided after examination of the relative risks of operating with a low level of stocks and the costs of restricting allocations to industry, thus losing valuable industrial output.

The problem is somewhat modified if we drop the assumption that the forecast trends of demand and supply are the same over the budget period. If, for example, although total output and consumption are expected to be in balance in the period, the rate of output is expected to rise more rapidly than the rate of consumption, that is the rate of output is below that of consumption at the beginning of the period but above it at the end, then we should be content to enter the period with a comparatively low level of stocks in the knowledge that the rate of fall of stocks would probably diminish and eventually be transformed into a rate of increase. Further, provided that there was no immediate prospect of the rate of consumption catching up with the rate of output in the period after that of the budget, a comparatively slow rate of stock building would be quite sufficient in the latter half of the budget period. Attitudes both to the level of stocks and to its rate of change would be changed in the opposite direction if the rate of output was increasing less rapidly over the period under review than was consumption.

The situation becomes more involved if, although total output and consumption are expected to be in balance for a year, separate budgets are prepared for two periods of six months. The coal 'year' is divided into the summer period (May to October) and the winter period (November to April). In the former, coal output exceeds consumption and stocks can be built up, while during the winter coal output is less than consumption and stocks are run down. If as the result of a severe winter coal stocks are brought down to a very low level by the beginning of the summer, careful consideration will have to be given to the rate at which they should be rebuilt during the summer months. The loss of industrial production resulting from reduced summer coal allocations must be weighed against the risks of entering the next winter with lower stocks than usual.

If superimposed on the normal seasonal movement for output is an expected rising trend exceeding that of consumption, then the need to rebuild stocks in summer is less pressing because there is likely to be a smaller drawing on stocks in the winter than if trends of output and consumption were approximately the same.

There can thus be no ready answer to the problem of stocks. It is an oversimplification to imply, as do the Coal Board, that the rebuilding of stocks during the summer to a level of 20 million tons by the end of October should have precedence over current consumption.[1] Judgement based on a balanced view of possibilities is what is needed and not the arbitrary allocation of absolute priority to a single end. Nevertheless it is as well to remember that before the Second World War the existence of a substantial pool of unemployed miners enabled the output of coal to be varied fairly quickly in both directions in response to temporary changes in demand. Today elasticity can only be maintained in the short run if rather larger stocks are held or by the difficult device of varying the extent of Saturday working. If there is a reluctance on the part of consumers to build up stocks at times when the supplies of coal are temporarily ample, either encouragement can be given, as at present, by offering house coal at lower prices in the summer, or the Government can itself assume the responsibility for holding reserve stocks.

The further abandonment of our simplifying assumption and the entry into the picture of both imports and exports makes the decision-maker's choice at once wider and more embarrassing. The process of balancing a period's budget must now be achieved by a simultaneous juggling with possible variations in the rate of fall (or rise) of stocks, the flow of coal to various kinds of consumer and the rate of exporting or importing of coal. The costs, both financial and real, and risks of varying one item must be compared with those that will result from the necessary compensating adjustments to be made to other items. This would be difficult enough even if coal could be regarded as a homogeneous commodity, but in fact the budget must attempt to equate the supplies of and the demands for different grades of coal. A restriction of the supplies of coal for electricity generation, even if desirable or possible, would on the whole release only low-grade coal for other users. However, the global coal budget cannot be broken down simply into a number of distinct sub-budgets for different grades of coal, since some degree of substitution of one grade for another in a particular use is usually possible, although the extent of possible substitution may vary widely

---

[1] See the Ridley report [59], pp. 118–19.

from user to user. Such a situation can justify the decision to import and export coal simultaneously.

In this complicated and hazardous balancing process, a sound judgement in estimating the real costs and risks of alternative courses of action is the main requirement. Statistics are helpful in deciding what will probably happen in the future on the basis of past experience. They can also assist in the making of subjective estimates of the chances that forecasts will be wrong. They enable a decision-maker to perceive clearly the implications of alternative courses of action and help to ensure that, where a variety of expedients are adopted, the resultant policy is internally consistent.

Once the necessary decisions have been taken and embodied in a balanced coal budget, those whose duty it is to oversee the implementation of the policy must keep a careful watch on actual events. It is necessary to observe the trends of actual output and consumption and the rate at which the level of stocks changes. This requires that due allowance be made for effect of normal seasonal variations in the weekly or monthly figures of output, consumption and stock change. An unexpectedly slow rate of stock build-up during the summer months may well be an indication of trouble ahead unless emergency action is taken. A fall in stocks during the winter may well justify larger allocations of coal for industry if the rate of fall is much slower than was anticipated. It is desirable that the public at large should also know what figures are the 'key' to the current coal situation, and that their attention should be diverted from an undue preoccupation with the level of stocks (and the week's output and consumption as compared with those of the previous year) to the broader picture.

A TEST CASE: THE FUEL CRISIS OF 1947

The point we have so far reached may be summarized as follows. There are on the whole plenty of reliable coal statistics for the past; in fact, so many as almost to confuse the mind and judgement. Much attention has to be given to estimating for future periods; here uncertainty necessarily comes in, and the size of stocks is important. But it is the *trend* of stocks, or the *trend* of production and consumption, which matters. Despite all the wealth of statistics, mistakes can be made by concentrating on the wrong ones—hence the importance of skilled presentation.

The process, and the dangers, can be illustrated by examining what happened in 1947—a time when coal planning was publicly revealed to an unusual extent. The end of 1946 saw distributed stocks of coal at the low level of 8·3 million tons, that is 4 million tons lower than the year before, despite an increase in output for the year of 6·5 million tons. Stocks continued to fall and stood at 5·5 million tons by the end of that month of industrial dislocation, February 1947. On the eve of the presentation of the summer coal budget by the late Sir Stafford Cripps, then President of the Board of Trade, *The Economist* newspaper declared (8 March): 'The first task in the summer months must be to build up stocks not by a mere 4 million tons or so as in the previous years but by at least 12 million tons.'[1] Two days later Sir Stafford Cripps also showed himself preoccupied with the problem of stock rebuilding and said: '...the best we can do this year is to make that [i.e. present stocks] up to 15 million tons by 15 November. Ideally it should be more—another 3 million to 5 million tons; but if we were to try and make it all up in this six months, it would mean so little left for industry that the position would be made impossible.' The details of the balanced coal budget for the period 1 May to 31 October are shown in Table 1.

The restrictions on allocations of coal to industry which the figure of 17·6 million tons implied were extremely severe. Industry was only to receive about two-thirds of its estimated requirements when running full out. The gas and electricity public utilities were, however, to be allotted sufficient coal for full industrial use 'consistent with allocation of solid fuel to industry'. Restrictions on domestic and non-industrial users of coal were to be continued throughout the summer and it was hoped by this means to save 80,000 tons a week, that is about 2 million tons over the period. A 10 % cut was to be imposed on railway passenger services compared with those of the summer of 1946, and in addition the introduction of summer services was not to take place until 1 June instead of 1 May as customary.

Comment in the ensuing debate in the House of Commons, while often angry about the manner in which the difficulties had been allowed to develop, did not appear seriously to question the Government's proposals for dealing with it. Mr Churchill, after quoting Mr Horner's speech in Edinburgh in October 1946 to the effect that a deficiency of 5 million tons of coal for industry would mean unemployment for 1 million people, went on to say: 'In January or February you must always make sure that you will be able, by the winter, to build up your stocks to the normal 18 million tons of coal or thereabouts, so that you do not drop below the distributional minimum on account of any extra winter consumption.'[2] Another Member of Parliament said: 'We must not start next winter, remembering the vagaries of our climate, with a lower stock of coal than 14 million or 15 million tons.'[3]

---

[1] This was reckoned to be feasible even after allowing 9 million tons to go as exports or bunkers and letting summer inland consumption stand at 100 million tons.

[2] See *Hansard* for 12 March 1947.

[3] See *Hansard* for 12 March 1947: Mr Bernard Taylor.

Table 1. *Summer coal budget*, 1947: 10 *March* 1947

(Period: 1 May to 31 October 1947)

Supplies	Forecast for summer 1947 (million tons)	Consumption	Forecast (allocation for summer 1947) (million tons)	Actual summer 1946 (million tons)
Deep-mined coal	83	Stocking up	10	(3·7)
Opencast coal	6	Electricity	11·8	(11·6)
		Gas	9·7	(10·2)
		Coke ovens, supplying town gas	5·2	··
		Water	0·2	··
		Railways	7·0	(7·5)
		Colliery consumption	5·3	(5·2)
		Miners' coal	2·1	(2·2)
		Merchants' disposal:		
		House coal	12·8	(12·8)
		Others	1·2	(1·2)
		Larger non-industrial consumers	1·5	··
		Northern Ireland	1·2 ⎫	
		Coastwise bunkers	0·5 ⎪	
		Service Departments	0·5 ⎬	(4·6)
		Miscellaneous	1·3 ⎭	
		Iron and steel		
		Coke ovens not supplying gas	} 17·6	(19·9)
		Other industries		
			87·9	
		Exports and bunkers	3·1	
			91·0	
		Saving by coal-oil conversion	−2·0	
	Total 89·0	Total	89·0	

Sources. *Hansard, The Economist.*   ·· = not available.

However, soon afterwards the full import of the proposed coal allocations on industrial production began to be realized. '...The austerity coal supplies now budgeted for industry this summer will involve the direst consequences for the nation'[1] in the shape of losses of steel output, of cotton supplies and of export earnings. The possibility of getting greater coal supplies was discussed. Imports of coal were mentioned, while the Federation of British Industries and the Trade Union Congress recommended that the coal 'target' for the calendar year be raised

[1] *The Economist*, 5 April 1947.

from 200 million tons to 220 million tons. The next step was to question the basis of the forecasts of coal output. It was certainly true that the trend of output was rising; in the first 17 weeks of the year up to the end of April output was over 3 million tons greater than in the same period of 1946 and this despite an estimated loss of nearly 900,000 tons owing to weather and transport difficulties. But, on the other hand, at the beginning of May the miners were to start working a five-day week and it was possibly wishful thinking to argue, as did *The Economist*, that miners would thereafter work five full shifts a week instead of only four and a half.

Prospects were however brightening, and comment became more balanced. In the middle of April coal allocations for industry were raised by 100,000 tons a week until the end of May. At about the same time *The Economist* remarked: 'Plainly it would be folly to gamble on the chance of any substantial import of coal from the United States this year. But equally it would be folly to prevent industry restoring its full rate of output as soon as coal output permits, even if that does entail some risk for next winter.'

On 1 May Sir Stafford Cripps announced revised coal allocations. After drawing attention to the fact that the manpower position of the coal industry had improved since his statement on 10 March, he said: '...there is a clear risk in planning allocations to industry at a higher level than I then indicated, in view of the uncertainty which must remain concerning output during the summer. On the other hand, the Government cannot fail to be impressed by the fact that supplies at such a level would not only cause industrial dislocation during the summer, but would also create shortages of materials and components which must seriously prejudice the operation of industry through the next winter.'[1]

Over the period from 1 June to 31 October 1947 industry was now to receive supplies of coal equal to the consumption of the same period in 1946, subject to the necessary adjustments for new factories, oil conversion, etc. There was to be a special extra allocation for building-material industries. Firms were required to build up a stock equal to three weeks' winter requirements by the end of October. Firms that succeeded in stocking more than this would not lose thereby on their winter allocations, but those that failed would receive no extra winter coal. In all, industry was to receive about 85 % of its solid fuel requirements. Over the full six-months period from 1 May to 31 October industry would be able to consume 21 million tons of coal as against the original allowance of 17·6 million tons and was instructed to put a further 4 million tons into stock.

[1] *Hansard* for 1 May 1947.

During the early part of the summer the manpower position continued to improve, and so also did figures of output per man-shift. With the introduction of the five-day week the average number of shifts worked per week fell, thus offsetting in part the other favourable developments. As the summer drew on, negotiations took place between the National Coal Board and the National Union of Mineworkers on the question of increasing the length of each shift by half an hour or of working alternate Saturdays.

Table 2. *Winter coal budget*, 1947–8: 14 *October* 1947

(Period: 1 November 1947 to 30 April 1948)

Supplies	Forecast for winter 1947–8 (million tons)	Consumption	Forecast (allocation for winter 1947–8) (million tons)	Actual winter 1946–7 (million tons)
Deep-mined coal	97	Electricity	16·45	(15·50)
		Gas	13·75	(12·70)
Opencast coal	4·25	Coke ovens	10·75	(9·70)
Running down stocks (this allows stocks to fall to 6·5 mn. tons by 1 May 1948)	8·75	Railways	7·50	(7·70)
		Colliery consumption and miners' coal	8·70	(8·40)
		Merchants' disposals:		
		House coal	16·90	(16·30)
		Other coal	1·30	(1·38)
		Miscellaneous*	8·34	(8·34)
		Large industrial consumers	23·51†	(19·87)
			107·20	(99·89)
		Exports and bunkers	2·80‡	(2·90)
	110·0	Total	110·0	(102·79)

* Includes water, Northern Ireland, non-industrial consumers, coastwise bunkers, and small and seasonal industrial consumers.
† Oil conversion to save the equivalent of 0·90 million tons.
‡ All bunkers. [Note: 6 million tons of exports to Europe in 1948 had been promised.]

Source. Keesing's Contemporary Archives (press reports).

On 14 October Mr Gaitskell, the Minister of Fuel and Power, gave details of the winter coal budget for the period from 1 November 1947 to the end of May 1948. He reported that stocks of coal had reached about 15 million tons and that in all 9 million tons of coal had been added to stocks during the summer months, compared with 4 million tons in 1946. The higher rate of stock-building had been achieved by the elimination of 2 million tons of exports, by lowering inland consumption by 1·6 million tons, and by an increase in supplies of 1·3 million tons, of which nearly half were imports.[1] In the calendar year 1947 it was now expected that output would amount to 197 million tons against a 'target' figure of 200 million tons. The details of the winter coal budget are shown in Table 2.

Domestic consumers were getting an increase in coal supplies only sufficient to allow for the number of new households. The supplies of gas and electricity to non-industrial users were to be 10 % less than the year before. Allowing for oil conversion, industry was to get an increase of 23 % above the previous winter's figures, but 2·2 million tons of winter consumption was to be met by running down the stocks held by industry. The extra supplies of coal to the coke ovens would mean that the supplies of coke to the iron and steel industry could be increased by 25 % and to the rest of industry by 12½ %.

From 1 November the mines began working extra Saturday shifts at some pits and longer shifts at others. By the beginning of December things were going sufficiently well for exports of coal to be restarted, and regular exports began on 1 January 1948. The winter coal budget allocation of 112,000 tons a week for exports and bunkers was raised to 200,000 tons a week. At about the same time *The Economist* reported that Mr Horner hoped for an output of 250 million tons and pre-war exports within two years, and commented that 'he is not given to making incautious predictions'.

The history of this period is interesting because it shows how comment was at first concentrated on a single, and apparently definite, figure— the beginning-of-winter stock level; measures threatening severe dislocation were adopted, and then relaxed as it was realized that the trends of output and consumption did not necessitate them. But if the Government were excessively pessimistic, outside comment was often unduly hopeful—it implied trends of manpower, attendance and productivity which were not likely. The whole process would have been much more realistic if the future had been described, not by single 'best estimates' but by 'ranges of possibility' (so that the risk of the worst could have been consciously related to the chance of the best), and if attention had been directed to trends instead of static period-estimates. The lesson is that, even where there are plenty of facts, their right presentation is vital.

STATISTICS AND LONG-TERM POLICY

With supplies insufficient or barely sufficient at the arranged price, short-term planning can be concerned with physical quantities; price can be assumed constant or of secondary importance. But in the long

---

[1] Output for the full six months of summer was in fact 1·6 million tons higher than the year before.

run we cannot suppose this to be so, and we meet again the dilemma of Chapter IV: we are uncertain about future price policies (partly because we lack the facts necessary to judge between alternatives): we are uncertain about the reactions of price on demand and supply (partly because there has been no free market in recent years). The wild divergence of different statistical estimates in this field is an instructive example of apparent definiteness concealing varied and muddled assumptions.

In drawing up a long-term plan of development for the coal industry, the first step is a forecast of the level of demand for, say, 15 years ahead. After such a forecast has been made, the investment plans and schemes of reorganization can be drawn up with the aim of achieving this output at the lowest possible cost. Forecasting ahead such a long way is clearly an extremely tricky business, and the figures obtained will be subject to wide margins of error. The main requirement is, however, a clear indication of the direction in which things should start moving, while the distance to be traversed in the time is a subsidiary, though not unimportant, matter.

In the National Coal Board's *Plan for Coal*[1] forecasts are made of the annual demand for coal in the period 1961–5. A general account of the technique used and of the conclusions reached is given in Chapters III, 'Demand', and V, 'How the plan was made', of the National Coal Board's publication. No useful purpose would be served by recapitulating the same story here. More recently the same problem has been examined by the Ridley Committee in its report on National Policy for the Use of Fuel and Power Resources[2] and forecasts have been made of the annual demand in the period 1959–63.

In both cases the techniques used give rise to certain doubts about their adequacy. In the short run the projection of past trends is a valid and, indeed, perhaps the only means of making forward estimates, for the crystal-gazer must assume the continued operation of most of the various forces at work in the past. The same device, even when coupled with certain assumptions about the likely rate of increase of industrial production and of efficiency of fuel utilization, is much less defensible in the longer run. For now demand will be shaped also by the pricing policies pursued not only by the National Coal Board but also by the Gas Boards, the Electricity Authority and the oil industry. If we consider coal as a homogeneous product it might possibly be argued that the total demand for coal, given the level of oil and coal prices, is independent of the relation existing between the prices of gas, electricity and coal. We could then go on to say that the difficulty of predicting the

---

[1] [83].   [2] Ridley report [59].

future relative levels of coal and oil prices, or the sensitivity of demand to any charges that may occur, precludes our taking account of the influence of prices in our calculations. Once, however, we acknowledge the existence of different grades of coal, and different places of use, such a line of argument wears somewhat thin. The National Coal Board must plan its future organization on the basis of forecasts of demand for different grades of coal in different places, and this it cannot do unless there is detailed forecasting of the demand of the different users. There can surely be little doubt that the re-casting of electricity tariffs might well result in a marked change both in the amount of coal used for electricity generation and in that used by gasworks. It is difficult to see therefore how demand can be treated realistically when it is assumed to be independent of relative prices.

The National Coal Board does recognize that the demand for the different grades of coal will depend on their relative prices, but it does not go on to examine the implications of the fact that such demand is often a derived one, which in turn depends on the price policy of some other public utility.

To recognize the dependence of demand upon price is one thing and to take it into account in forecasting is another. Two kinds of knowledge are necessary before this can be done. First an analysis of the market demand for different sorts of fuel must be conducted in order to determine the elasticity of their demand with respect to their own prices and to the prices of their rivals. Secondly an attempt must be made to discover what methods of pricing are likely to be used by the various parts of the fuel and power industry in the period for which forecasts are required. Taken together these two kinds of research represent a formidable task, but something on these lines is clearly required.

If we perforce ignore the complications introduced by having to consider prices, the job of forecasting becomes somewhat less intricate but still retains great difficulties. The authors have been told of unpublished analyses of the relationship between the consumption of primary fuels and national income or industrial production. The results indicate, for instance, that a 4 % increase in real national income is associated with an increase of about $2\frac{1}{2}$ % in the consumption of primary fuel. These somewhat chancy calculations are consistent both with the experience of individual countries over time and with variations between countries at a given time. There is, however, a danger that such calculations aggregate together too many varied factors—such as the growth of petroleum consumption for motor transport, and changing habits in heating houses—to be useful. Further, should not the factors assisting the progressive improvement in the efficiency of fuel utilization be carefully studied on their own?

In order to emphasize the part which judgement must play in making this sort of prediction, it is worth while comparing a number of different forecasts made with the use of presumably much the same basic material. As a starting point we may look first at the forecasts of the Ridley Committee given in Table 3.

Table 3. *Annual fuel and power consumption in the United Kingdom: estimates for* 1951 *and forecasts for* 1959–63 *made by the Ridley Committee*

(Million tons of coal and coal equivalent)

Sector	Coal directly used and indirectly used as coke, gas and electricity		Oil fuels (excluding road transport fuels)		Total fuel consumption	
	1951	1959–63	1951	1959–63	1951	1959–63
Domestic	59·7	66·3*	0·7	1·1*	60·4	67·4*
Iron and steel	32·3	44·57 ⎱ †	1·5	2·7 ⎱ †	33·8	47·2 ⎱ †
Other industry	59·4	69·5 ⎰	4·1	7·1 ⎰	63·5	76·6 ⎰
Commercial	11·9	13·6‡	0·2	1·0‡	12·1	14·6‡
Public authorities	11·6	12·4	0·2	0·2	11·8	12·6
Railways	15·7	15·4	0·1	0·3	15·8	15·7
Collieries	12·1	9·1	—	—	12·1	9·1
Northern Ireland	2·8	3·1	—	—	2·8	3·1
Others§	1·9	2·1	—	—	1·9	2·1
Total	207·4‖	236·0‖	6·8	12·4	214·2	248·4

* A suppressed demand for coal of 5 million tons is assumed for 1951, and it is further assumed that if this demand were met the demand for gas and electricity would be reduced by 1 million tons of coal equivalent. By 1961 it is assumed that heat comfort per head will increase by 10%, efficiency of use will increase by 5%, population will increase by 1 million, and miners' coal will fall to 4 million tons.
† Industrial production is assumed to increase by 4% per annum cumulatively and fuel efficiency by 1% per annum.
‡ Consumption is assumed to increase by 1% per annum.
§ Losses in transit, stock changes unaccounted for, and any errors.
‖ Including, for 1951, 1·1 million tons of coal equivalent for water power used in generating electricity and 0·7 million tons for oil used in gas-making; in 1959–63 1·9 and 1·6 million tons respectively.
Source. Ridley report [59], pp. 5, 6.

The forecasts given for the annual consumption of coal in 1959–63 are markedly sensitive to changes in the assumptions about the rate of increase of industrial production and of fuel efficiency. The effect of such changes on the Ridley Committee's forecasts and a comparison with forecasts made by the Federation of British Industries[1] and by the National Coal Board in its *Plan for Coal* are illustrated in Table 4.

[1] See Ridley report [59], Appendix xii(a), pp. 216–17.

Table 4. *Forecasts of annual coal consumption in the United Kingdom*

(Million tons of coal)

| Class of consumer | 1951 actual | 1959–63 Ridley Committee | | | 1961–5 | |
		I	II	III	Federation of British Industries	National Coal Board
Industry	46·3	40·7*	47·1	54·4*	56	..
Electricity	35·4	45·0*	48·3	52·1*	63	48†
Domestic	30·0	30·6	30·6	30·6	40	..
Railways	14·1	13·7	13·7	13·7	15	..
Miscellaneous‡	11·9	10·8	10·8	10·8	13	..
Total above	137·7	140·8	150·5	161·6	187	138–145
Gas and coke ovens	52·3	65·1*	70·5	76·5*	64	56–58
Miners' coal and collieries	15·6	11·5	11·5	11·5	12	11–12
Grand total	205·6	217·4*	232·5	249·6*	263	205–215

·· = not available.

Notes. Assumptions for Ridley Committee forecasts:

I. Industrial production rising by 2% per annum and fuel efficiency by ¼% per annum in the iron and steel industry and ½% in the rest of industry.

II. As in Table 3 on p. 47—that is, a 4% rise per annum in the volume of industrial production, coupled with a rise in efficiency of fuel utilization of ¾% per annum for the iron and steel industry and 1% for the rest of industry.

III. Industrial production rising by 6% per annum and fuel efficiency by 1½% per annum in the iron and steel industry and 1½% in the rest of industry.

* Authors' forecasts based on Ridley Committee's assumptions and forecasts.

† See *Plan for Coal* [83], para. 88.

‡ Includes Commercial, Public Authorities, Northern Ireland and Others (see Table 3).

In order to estimate the total demand for British coal output, some forecasts must also be made of export demand. The Ridley Committee estimated that the total demand for exports and bunkers in 1951 was of the order of 26–31 million tons, that is there was an unsatisfied export demand of 13–18 million tons. Both the Ridley Committee and the Federation of British Industries have fought shy of investigating future export demand and have simply accepted the Coal Board's forecast of 25–35 million tons a year by 1961–5. The Coal Board discussed export prospects in some detail in their *Plan for Coal*[1] and readily acknowledged that such demand is much more sensitive to price than is inland demand. Whatever happens to the overall demand and supply of coal in Western Europe in the next five years, it is hoped that demand for special coals such as steam coal and anthracite will be well maintained. If such hopes are not justified, the Coal Board's development plans will be seriously upset, since investment to the tune of £97 million[2] (at 1950 prices) in the

[1] See *Plan for Coal* [83], p. 23, paras. 92–5.

[2] The total investment in collieries over the same period is placed at £520 million.

period 1950–65 was intended to be undertaken in the high-cost South Wales collieries in order to satisfy prospective export demand.

This great variation in estimates for the future raises questions about long-term investment planning, rather than about statistics. But it suggests the way in which statistical knowledge will have to move. It will be necessary to look out for opportunities of obtaining knowledge about elasticities of demand and supply of coal, about the costs and savings involved in further improvement of fuel utilization, about the relation of coal consumption to industrial output in a changing industrial structure, and so on; in fact, there must be research to give the Ridley Committee's broad assumptions more backing in fact. Furthermore, there is need for thought about the ranges of possibility in the future; it is folly to relate an expensive investment programme to a single 'best estimate' of future consumption at an unknown price. Finally, the *progress* of the investment programme needs to be examined in relation to the changing needs of the coal market—to make sure that plans have not lost touch with reality. There is scope for plenty of economic research here, though it may not involve much extra collection of information. Until it has been undertaken, statistical estimates for the distant future should be presented in a way which reminds the reader that they are, for the most part, mere exercises in guesswork and arithmetic.

CONCLUSIONS

What are the morals of the discussion? There would appear to be two major ones. The first is that no assemblage of figures about the past, however reliable or however comprehensive, can provide a certain guide about future events. To move from past history to prediction of the future, assumptions must be made about the nature of the causes of the pattern of past events and the extent to which these causes will operate in the future.

The second moral is this: even when forecasts of the quantitive aspects of future events have been made on certain assumptions, this new set of figures does not tell the policy-maker the right thing to do. All such forecasts can accomplish is the illumination of the consequences and the risks of a number of alternative policies (for example alternative price policies). Between such alternatives the policy-maker must himself judge. The forecasts may help him to give appropriate weight to opposing considerations, but the responsibility for evolving a balanced policy is his alone.

Two riders may be linked to this second moral. Where the maker of policy must lean heavily on statistical advisers for information but must himself decide the policy, it is essential that he be able himself to think 'statistically'—that is, in terms of probability distributions. By this we mean not that he must himself be a trained statistician but that his approach to affairs in general must be statistical in essence. In a world where the future is always uncertain to a greater or lesser degree, there should be no room for an administrator whose outlook is narrowly deterministic.

The second rider concerns not only the makers of policy but the informed public who are trying to understand what is going on. We have indicated that for the policy-maker statistics alone are not enough; judgement is the major requirement and this depends on the possession of a great deal of knowledge, not all susceptible of condensation into numbers. At present the public are not provided with such knowledge in the case of the coal industry. They are given the figures—perhaps too many figures—but their understanding is not aided by skilled presentation and by published interpretations by people with extensive qualitative knowledge of the coal industry. Maybe the press should take action to provide such informed comment, but in the event it does not and the remedy lies in the hands of those within or reigning over the industry itself.

We cannot ask the coal industry for more statistics, but we can and should demand that it should use more care in presenting them and provide supplementary information of a qualitative nature so that the published figures can be properly used and understood.

CHAPTER VI

THE DEVELOPMENT AREAS

During and since the Second World War Britain has seen a much increased State participation in the location of industry. This has taken two forms: first, the planning restrictions, designed to protect amenities and secure the balanced development of communities: secondly, the policies designed to direct industry into areas thought to be liable to heavy unemployment. It would be interesting to examine statistical needs in deciding industrial location, both from the point of view of the State and from that of the individual industrialist; but general location policy is a subject which needs further research before anything useful can be said about its statistical foundations. This chapter is confined to the policy of directing industry to the Development Areas, and in particular to two questions: how are the limits of the Development Areas to be defined, and what kind of industry is to receive special encouragement to go to a Development Area?

There is a quick superficial answer to both these questions: the Development Areas are in the main well-defined areas of heavy unemployment before 1939: and any industry not firmly tied to another place is encouraged to site new plant in one of the areas. If this is all that can be said, it is clear that the role of statistics in forming policy is negligible. But even if the superficial view were true, it would be interesting to inquire whether the factual basis exists, or could exist, for a more scientific and discerning policy.

HISTORICAL BACKGROUND

In the period between the two World Wars considerable national anxiety was caused by the existence of stagnant pools of exceptionally heavy unemployment in the so-called Special Areas. New industry was apparently drifting to the midlands and to the south, thus reinforcing the prosperity of these already relatively prosperous areas. Large cities were growing into larger 'conurbations', but there did not appear to be any automatic mechanism which ensured the birth of new towns containing a balanced community. Those new towns that appeared tended to be dormitory suburbs.

Certain stop-gap measures, which need not concern us here, were applied to the Special Areas, while the need for a deeper examination of the general problem was recognized by the setting up in 1937 of the

Royal Commission on the Distribution of the Industrial Population (the Barlow Commission). This Commission was 'to inquire into the causes which have influenced the present geographical distribution of the industrial population of Great Britain and the probable direction of any change in that distribution in the future; to consider what social, economic or strategical disadvantages arise from the concentration of industries or of the industrial population in large towns or in particular areas of the country; and to report what remedial measures if any should be taken in the national interest.'

Early in the Second World War the Barlow Commission made its report.[1] Although the Commission was divided on certain matters, there was unanimous agreement that 'the objectives of national action should be:

'(a) Continued and further redevelopment of congested urban areas, where necessary.

'(b) Decentralisation or dispersal, both of industries and industrial population, from such areas.

'(c) Encouragement of a reasonable balance of industrial development, so far as possible, throughout the various divisions or regions of Great Britain, coupled with appropriate diversification of industry in each division or region through the country.'[2]

In 1944 the Government's White Paper on *Employment Policy*[3] set out its attitude to the problem of the distribution of industry and foreshadowed much of the subsequent legislation. The White Paper stated (p. 11) that the Government proposed 'to attack the problems of local unemployment in three ways:

'(a) By so influencing the location of new enterprises as to diversify the industrial composition of areas which are particularly vulnerable to unemployment.

'(b) By removing obstacles to the transfer of workers from one area to another, and from one occupation to another.

'(c) By providing training facilities to fit workers from declining industries for jobs in expanding industries.'

At the end of the war the Board of Trade was allotted the task of 'securing the proper distribution of industry' under the Distribution of Industry Act, 1945. To achieve this object the Board of Trade was given certain powers in the Development Areas[4] designated by the Act, 'for the purpose of facilitating the provision of premises needed for meeting the requirements of industrial undertakings (including requirements

---

[1] [56].   [2] Barlow report [56], pp. 201–2.   [3] [58].

[4] The old Special Areas plus some other districts. Towards the end of the war there were clear indications of returning unemployment (though on a small scale) in the same areas which had suffered heavy unemployment before the war.

arising from the needs of persons employed or to be employed therein)'.[1] These powers included the compulsory purchase of land, the erection of buildings on such land, and the provision of financial assistance to trading or industrial estate companies, to industrial undertakings, and for the improvement of basic services.

The Development Areas were defined as those areas of the country where 'the distribution of industry is such that...there is likely to be a special danger of unemployment.'[2] The Board of Trade was enabled to add areas to the list of Development Areas or to remove areas, as the President thought fit, subject to his acting jointly with the Secretary of State in relation to any area in Scotland.

In general any person contemplating 'the erection of an industrial building forming part of a new industrial unit' of which the aggregate floor space exceeded 10,000 square feet was required to notify the Board of Trade of his intention and to give details of 'the proposed situation of the building, the industrial process to be carried on therein, the estimated aggregate floor space thereof, and the estimated number of men and of women to be employed.'[3] The provision applied to new industrial building in any part of the United Kingdom.

The details of the provisions of the Town and Country Planning Act, 1947, which came into operation on 1 July 1948, are not relevant to our main theme. One purpose of the Act was, however:

'To bring all development under control by making it, with certain exceptions, subject to the permission of a local planning authority or of central government.'[4]

To this end the Act amended certain sections of the Distribution of Industry Act of 1945 and laid down that any application to a local planning authority for permission to develop land by the erection, extension, alteration or re-erection of an industrial building of over 5,000 square feet must be accompanied by a Board of Trade Industrial Development Certificate to the effect that the proposed development was consistent with the proper distribution of industry. Before this, industrial development exceeding 5,000 square feet required approval of an interdepartmental Distribution of Industry Panel; the new system concentrated in the Board of Trade the responsibility which had previously been collective. This involved the repeal and supersession of the notification provision of the Distribution of Industry Act, 1945, and it has not been an unqualified success. Previously the officials of the Board of Trade might exert their influence before a business man's plans had become too definite, but the detail required in an application for an Industrial Development Certificate may mean that in some cases

---

[1] [55], Section 1.   [2] [55], Section 7(2).
[3] [55], Section 9.   [4] *Town and Country Planning, 1943–1951* [71], p. 10.

the project has reached an advanced stage before the Board hears about it.

It should be realized that a building, or an extension to an existing building, of which the floor space does not exceed 5,000 square feet or, in the case of a series of extensions, 5,000 square feet in any three years, does not require such a certificate. Thus an establishment with many buildings possesses a freedom denied to smaller concerns. Nor is there any restriction on acquiring existing premises, unless planning permission is required for a change of use.

The Distribution of Industry Act, 1950 strengthened the powers of the Board of Trade in the Development Areas. The Act made 'further provision for the acquisition of land, creation of easements and carrying out of work in development areas,' and authorized 'the Board of Trade to make grants in exceptional cases in connection with the establishment in, or transfer to, development areas of industrial undertakings, and to make grants or loans to housing associations for the provision of dwellings in development areas.'[1] There was also provision for making payments towards the cost of removal and resettlement of key workers and their dependants.[2]

It can be seen from this survey[3] that the Board of Trade's powers of direction and persuasion are two-fold: it can refuse an industrialist a Development Certificate for any area; and it can offer certain facilities and advantages in the Development Areas, not available elsewhere. But the industrialist who has gone to a lot of trouble to prepare an application for a Development Certificate for one area may give up in disgust if he is refused—hence the importance of early, informal contact: or he may join in the considerable industrial mobility between existing premises.

DEFINING THE DEVELOPMENT AREAS

Clearly the President of the Board of Trade has in his gift a considerable privilege, in the designation of an area as a Development Area, for which there is (in fact) considerable competition. But the policy would be frustrated if the total size of the Areas was too large, for the benefits would be too thinly spread. How is an area where 'the distribution of industry is such that there is likely to be a special danger of unemployment' to be defined?

The corresponding statistical problem is to find data which throw light on the future economic prospects of an area. Its past employment

---

[1] [55 a], Preamble.   [2] [55 a], Section 4.
[3] The legislation described relates to Great Britain. Northern Ireland, with a much heavier unemployment rate than the Development Areas, is outside its scope: local legislation provides somewhat fuller assistance to industry in the region.

history is clearly relevant, and unemployment figures for small districts are available in great detail. But this is not enough: a short history of unemployment in the recent past (for example in Lancashire in 1952) does not give rise to an expectation of 'a special danger of unemployment' unless there is reason to expect it to continue or recur: on the other hand, a long pre-war history of unemployment (for example in South Wales) was related to very different economic conditions. It is salutary to remember that the great troubles of the Special Areas were the depression in heavy industries and the decline of coal; it is a little odd, at first sight, that they should need special treatment at a time of boom in heavy industries and manpower shortage in coal.

The second type of data which can be examined is the existing industrial or employment structure of the area, and the extent of its concentration on a few industries. It is possible, within the departments, to assemble employment data for small areas. But the mere fact of concentration, though it may increase risks, does not of itself create a special danger of unemployment. Large parts of the country have their economic activity concentrated on agriculture and its ancillary trades; but this is not, at the present day, regarded as creating a risk of unemployment. The types of concentration which are dangerous are:

(i) On a declining trade, no expanding trade being present and able to absorb the labour displaced.

(ii) On a trade liable to wide fluctuations.

One possible line of inquiry, therefore, is to make a general survey of the whole industrial structure of the area; to assemble statistics about the demand for the products of the area, its competitors in trade, and the plans or forecasts of its industrialists. In London and in the regional offices of the Board of Trade surveys have been prepared in large numbers. They attempt to analyse: 'Variations in the industrial structure of regions and sub-regions and the factors underlying them; differences in industrial specialisation and diversification between and within regions and explanations of such differences; divergencies in the degree of vulnerability to structural and localised unemployment as between areas; the distinctive industrial, economic, social and physical characteristics of the Development Areas; the industrial facilities and basic services; the constitution and geographical distribution of industrial population, labour supplies, industrial sites; the availability of factory premises, housing and general amenities.'[1] We shall discuss these surveys further below.

Another line of inquiry is into the characteristics of the people of the area. Is the population growing or declining? What is the rate of migration, and where do people migrate to? This is information which is not likely to be immediately available, but which is needed if one is to assess

[1] [57], p. 33.

how far unemployment may be lessened by shifts of population. What are the skills of the unemployed workers, or those in danger of unemployment, and what chance is there of their being suitable for other industries? What is the balance of employment between men and women, and is there evidence of a concealed reserve of married women who would like employment? How many people are suffering from industrial and other diseases, or are otherwise in need of special conditions of employment? Statistics on matters such as these will help, not only in assessing the seriousness of the economic problems of an area, but in determining how much it could be helped by applying Development Area policy to it. And since industrialists can only be attracted if a fair choice of sites, labour and facilities can be offered, the 'special danger of unemployment' must exist, not in a single small town, but in a fair-sized district; and it must be fairly continuous throughout that district—small pockets of unemployment in a prosperous area are likely to disappear of their own accord.

In October 1948 the Board of Trade reported, as it was charged to do under the 1945 Act, on the desirability of removing any areas from the list of Development Areas, and also considered the cases for adding a number of different areas to this list. Two areas, Merseyside and part of the Highlands, were scheduled but none was discarded. In its report the Board discussed in the following terms the conditions that an area must satisfy before it could be scheduled as a Development Area:

'Before an area can be scheduled the Board of Trade must, by the terms of the Act, be satisfied that there is, or is likely to be, a special danger of unemployment in that area. This must mean in general that there is a danger of unemployment which is markedly more serious in relation to that area than in relation to most parts of the country. The existing rate of unemployment in the area is one of the most important factors to be considered. But there are others, such as the past history of the area, and the effects on the unemployment position in the area of any alterations, either in general conditions such as world demand, or in the demand for the products produced particularly in the area under consideration. The specific character of the unemployment problem must also be taken into account. In particular it is necessary to see whether there are sufficient employment opportunities for both men and women available. But in any case it can hardly be said that a special danger of unemployment exists unless both the following conditions obtain or will almost certainly obtain in the near future as a consequence of known factors—(1) that the average rate of unemployment is persistently high, (2) that the number of unemployed persons within the area is high in the aggregate.'[1]

[1] [57], p. 26.

Later on in the document the Board declares that small pockets of unemployment cannot be scheduled under the Act nor can a large area containing a number of small pockets of unemployment be so treated. In the discussion of the situation existing in the Scottish Highlands and Islands there occurs the statement: 'But the fact that the population has declined, and continues to decline, is by itself quite insufficient to bring the area within the ambit of the Distribution of Industry Act. What is significant is the unemployment position.'[1]

It can be seen that the Board's emphasis has been on the existing and past unemployment record of the area; and we have found no evidence that the more comprehensive statistical inquiries mentioned above (many of which are made by the Board's research staff) exert much influence on policy in this particular field. This seems to be an instance where the range of statistics which might be consulted as a background to a policy decision is so great that only the most obvious is chosen.

THE CHOICE OF INDUSTRY

The theory behind the choice of industry to be encouraged in Development Areas may be supposed to be that the new industry should be different from what is already there, both in its liability to booms and slumps and in the kind of employment which is offered. Hence there might be virtue in concentration on light consumer-goods industries, complementary to the existing capital-goods industries; these have the advantage of offering employment to women in areas where such employment has usually been limited. They may also (following past experience) be less liable to fluctuation, though they may include new and struggling firms which quickly disappear in bad times. But there is surely also much to be said for encouraging up-and-coming capital goods industries[2] to replace industries that are declining, whether these are concerned with capital, export or consumption goods. Even if it is true that capital goods industries will suffer more severely from slumps in the future, at least the young of this variety may lead the way to recovery.

The elaborate regional surveys described above could be brought into use as a means of judging what industries are to be encouraged. Analyses are also carried out by the regional staff of the Board of Trade of the situation existing in comparatively small districts, such as a town and that area of countryside the economic fate of which is closely linked with the fortunes of the town. These investigations necessarily require the close co-operation of the local representatives on the Distribution of Industry Panel of the Ministry of Housing and Local Government and

---

[1] [57], p. 31.   [2] Cairncross and Meier [90].

of the Ministry of Labour. As for the surveys for larger areas, the district's geography is described, and estimates are given of the size and structure of the existing insured and resident population together with forecasts of the changes that the future probably holds in store. The extent of and the form taken by recent industrial developments will be set out and the degree to which it has diminished the local unemployment problem or altered the proportion of local industry particularly dependent on a narrow range of markets will be assessed. Sometimes an attempt may be made to discover whether part of the resident population is forced through a paucity of local industry to seek work outside the district, or whether alternatively the labour force is reinforced by a daily influx of workers who cannot find houses nearer to their work. Where the under-employment of women is a cause for concern, the causes and severity of this problem may be investigated in detail.

The results yielded by these surveys should be of considerable value, whether or not the area concerned is likely to be eligible for the special treatment accorded to Development Areas. All applications for Industrial Development Certificates are intended to be examined on their individual merits against a background of the kind that such a survey can provide.

It is not possible to delimit with precision all the statistical information that can be used in the preparation of the surveys. At one time or another a very large proportion of the whole body of existing economic statistics, both official and otherwise, may be required to play a part. Nevertheless an enumeration can be made of a relatively small amount of statistical data which tends to be deployed frequently. This body of statistics consists of the following:

(i) (a) The number of unemployed.

(b) The number of outstanding vacancies.[1]

Both sets of figures are obtainable from the Ministry of Labour for each month, classified by Employment Exchange Areas in combination with industries.

(ii) (a) The insured population by industries for each Employment Exchange Area (or group of Areas).

(b) The resident and occupied populations; censuses and annual estimates by local authority areas. At a pinch some of these figures can be approximately redistributed by Employment Exchange Areas.

---

[1] Figures of outstanding vacancies are dangerous in that they are liable to sudden and not obviously explicable evaporation. Even so they are often used with the unemployment statistics to determine areas of labour 'shortage' and 'surplus'. Whether the figures of outstanding vacancies are regarded as useful or not seems to depend on the 'tightness' of the local labour position.

(*c*) Details of migration, so far as they can be supplied by the General Register Office.

(*d*) Projections of future population,[1] supplied by the General Register Office.

(iii) (*a*) The geographical distribution of new factory buildings for which Industrial Development Certificates have been granted;[2] the subsequent stages of such development, that is grant of planning permission or of a building licence.

(*b*) Employment potentially to be provided by the new industrial development in (iii) (*a*), and the employment so far provided.[3]

The Board of Trade also has access to the 'L' (Direct Employment) Returns of the Ministry of Labour, so that the numbers of workers employed by individual factories are known. This information is unfortunately now subject to the Statistics of Trade Act, 1947, and thus can only be used for internal purposes by the Board of Trade. Despite the fact that the Board of Trade itself organizes the Censuses of Production and of Distribution, the officials concerned with the distribution of industry do not have access to all the basic information derived therefrom.

Other sources of knowledge less regularly used are the *Housing Returns* and details of the quarterly census of the building labour force conducted by the Ministry of Works, Lloyd's Register shipbuilding returns, shipping movements at United Kingdom ports, coal and other production statistics, etc.

It would be helpful to the existing practice of compiling surveys if there was more information available about the current use of buildings, new and old, and both industrial and domestic. A partial remedy in respect of houses will be afforded when the detailed information derived from the 1951 Census of Population becomes available. At present the Board of Trade has no early information about changes in the use of existing industrial premises, and what knowledge there is available must be derived from an inspection of 'L' returns or from a perusal of the local press. If it were possible to maintain an up-to-date list of the use of all buildings in an area, many bodies both public and private would be saved from a great deal of work and difficulty; we shall return to this point in Chapter XII.

These area surveys have certain obvious uses. They enable the Board's officers in the regions to be well-informed about local industry, and able

[1] In regions where future migration is likely to be of considerable importance these projections are rarely used.

[2] In the Development Areas a careful record is kept of all forms of industrial development, and its scope is not restricted to that for which certificates are necessary.

[3] There is evidence that firms trying to enter the Development Areas tend to exaggerate the amount of employment eventually to be offered, while firms wishing to go to such areas as the Midlands tend to understate the same figures.

to give information about sites, labour prospects, etc., to enquiring industrialists. They provide reasons why Industrial Development Certificates should on occasion be refused, outside the Development Areas. But it seems to us probable that their influence on development *within* the Areas is slight and indirect, except perhaps in steering development to the blacker spots. The Board has not usually been in a position to pick and choose between different kinds of development; it has offered certain inducements, and has usually been glad if industrialists have been persuaded to take advantage of them. The Development Areas themselves have in some cases been more interested in their special employment needs (for example, more work for men) than in a general policy of diversification.

The information which is really relevant, therefore, is that which persuades private industry that it is profitable to set up in the Areas. This includes facts of the kind mentioned above—some of which may be passed on by the Board. But, much more importantly, it includes projections of what may happen to demand and to costs in the future. It is not the job of a Government department to make *detailed* projections of the future prospects of numerous trades; that is work which industry can do much better for itself. The statistical problem thus becomes that of giving industry reasonable access to information of use in judging future prospects; it is the problem of availability and presentation, discussed in Chapter XI.

Four additional types of information would help in guiding the growth of new industry in the Areas. One is more information about migration,[1] distinguishing what kinds of people move and how far they go; this could be obtained by a special sample survey. It would indicate how far it is necessary, because of labour immobility, to 'take the work to the workers'. The second is more research on the measurable social costs of allowing an area to decline; for instance, if a derelict mining village consists largely of cottages which require early rebuilding, there may be a strong case for doing the rebuilding elsewhere, near a suitable factory site—the money value of what would be abandoned would be small. The third type of knowledge which would be useful relates to the rate and direction of industrial growth of small areas. This could be obtained from the further analysis of the data collected in the past for the Censuses of Production. The publication of this information for recent years would, it is true, raise difficult problems of confidentiality,[2] but there could be little practical objection to legislation allowing the revelation of details about operations of particular firms more than, say, five years ago. Such analyses might be confined to areas the eligibility of which for scheduling as Development Areas was being reviewed.

[1] Newton and Jeffery [67] is a useful beginning.   [2] See Chapter XI, p. 132.

The fourth type of information, perhaps the most fundamental, relates to the experience of firms which have already set up works in Development Areas; or, more generally, to the costs of industrial movement and the factors which have to be taken into account in determining industrial location. Some valuable research in this difficult field has been undertaken at the National Institute of Economic and Social Research: reference may be made to occasional Papers XIV (*The Cost of Industrial Movement*, by W. F. Luttrell, 1952) and XV (*Costs in Alternative Locations: The Clothing Industry*, by D. C. Hague and P. K. Newman, 1952), and to the forthcoming final report, *Factory Location and Industrial Movement: A study of recent experience in Great Britain*. Other studies are in progress at the University of Birmingham.

But while better statistical and economic information might help in identifying industries likely to grow in a particular environment, no quantitative knowledge will help us much in picking out the scientific discoveries which will have an important effect on the technique of industrial production. Professors Cairncross and Meier have summarized the position in the following words:

'When we...consider...how such advances might be employed in order to accelerate industrial development, we can make no progress without a thorough knowledge of the growing points both in science and in industry. The human mind is limited in its power to keep track of new developments through the maze of technical and trade journals, and still more limited in its power to forecast the success or failure of developments that have not yet been put to the test of commercial profit or loss. The task of giving quantitative shape to such forecasts, and judging at what rate new industries might grow, what scale they might reach and what returns they might yield, both in wages and in profits, is peculiarly hazardous.'[1]

JUDGING THE RESULTS

The general economic prosperity of the Development Areas can be judged roughly by their unemployment rate—but only roughly, for they may have a peculiar distribution of workers by age and skill which makes it impossible to reduce unemployment as low as it is elsewhere in the country. There is no direct way of finding how far any improvement is due to general prosperity, private action, or good luck, and how far it is due to special State assistance. The direct employment provided by new firms, and their expected employment when in full operation, are recorded; but we do not know, of course, how much secondary employment they provide in the area.

A more refined judgement of the rightness of giving or continuing

[90], pp. 8-9.

special help to particular areas would be possible if we knew more about their incomes, the values of their product, and their patterns of expenditure. There are grave difficulties in assigning income to particular areas, because the usual primary source of information is from tax collection, and taxes are often collected in places different from those in which income first arises. Two inquiries in progress at the Department of Applied Economics, Cambridge are likely to give significant help. One is an attempt to construct, so far as possible, regional social accounts (by standard regions of the United Kingdom); the other is an experiment designed to find, by sampling, the main elements of the social accounts of a single county. But it will clearly be some time before the methodology so established can be successfully applied to a number of other areas.

CONCLUSION

This chapter gives an interesting example of the use of a great mass of statistical work to provide a general background to decision. The decisions made, whether Government or private, are based on many factors other than this background information—indeed, its direct use seems to be quite small. The question arises, therefore, whether statistical effort is here being wasted. We do not think that such waste can be definitely established, since the information collected has other uses, but it might well be desirable to give more attention to studying dynamic development instead of a static picture of the situation.

CHAPTER VII

AGRICULTURAL PRICE FIXING

In this chapter an examination will be made of the way in which statistics are used in the making of certain policy decisions about British agriculture. The decisions concerned are those made by the Government at the annual review and fixing of farm prices which has taken place in February of each year and at the special reviews which (under the Agriculture Act of 1947) may take place during the course of a year. It is not the purpose of this discussion to express views on the general wisdom of the policy initiated during the war and continued into peacetime by the 1947 Act. This is a matter for agricultural and other economists rather than for economic statisticians. Nor is it necessary to give a history of the stages by which the present procedure was evolved, for students interested in this evolution may refer to Professor E. F. Nash's essay on 'Wartime Control of Food and Agricultural Prices' in *Lessons of the British War Economy*[1] and to Mr R. J. Hammond's *Food*[2] (vol. 1).

The scope of the investigation undertaken here is limited to a brief account of the present procedure and an estimate of the importance of the part played by statistics in the process of price fixing. On the assumption that it is necessary for the Government of the day and the Ministry of Agriculture to implement the statutory provisions of the Agriculture Act of 1947, some attention will be paid to the adequacy of the statistical intelligence at present available. We shall find that the existing information is not entirely satisfactory, either in the extent of the field that it covers or in its reliability, and we shall suggest some improvements.

Where, as is true of the fixing of farm prices, the Government is negotiating on behalf of the community at large with a particular group of producers, who have the notable advantage of being well organized and at the same time control an extremely important sector of the country's economy, academic commentators will do well to exercise restraint and responsibility both in their analysis and in their recommendations. A destructive attack on the present methods, unless accompanied by detailed alternative proposals, would hardly assist either of the parties concerned to solve their problem.

[1] [93].   [2] [97].

THE REVIEW PROCEDURE

The general objectives of the Agriculture Act, 1947, are those of 'promoting and maintaining...a stable and efficient agricultural industry capable of producing such part of the nation's food and other agricultural produce as in the national interest it is desirable to produce in the United Kingdom, and of producing it at minimum prices consistently with proper remuneration and living conditions for farmers and workers in agriculture and an adequate return on capital invested in the industry' (Section 1, 1). To further these requirements the Government is empowered by the Act, and subsequent changes, to provide guaranteed prices and assured markets for cattle, sheep, pigs, milk, eggs, wheat, barley, oats, rye, potatoes, sugar beet and wool. These products taken together account, roughly speaking, for about 80 % of total agricultural output.

Under the Act the Government must, in consultation with representatives of agricultural producers, review each year the general profitability of the agricultural industry and its prospects for the ensuing years. The Ministers concerned in these discussions are the Minister of Agriculture and Fisheries and the Secretaries of State dealing with agriculture in Scotland and in Northern Ireland, while their opposite numbers are the representatives of the National Farmers' Union of England and Wales, the National Farmers' Union of Scotland and the Ulster Farmers' Union. After these negotiations have taken place and when the information brought to light during their progress has been considered, the Government finally fixes the prices of the so-called 'review' products.

It is desirable to describe the whole review procedure in rather more detail. A necessary preliminary to the whole business is the decision by the Government on the production of the various commodities that is required in the next two, or perhaps even the next three or four years. The spade work for this task is carried out by the Ministries of Agriculture and Food, the Treasury, the Central Economic Planning Staff and the Economic Section of the Cabinet Office, and the results of these official deliberations are submitted to Ministers for their approval. The decisions reached are clearly fundamental to all of the subsequent negotiations with the farmers' representatives. It would be of considerable interest to examine the part played by statistics either actively or as passive background material in arriving at the desired production objectives, but it is not possible to pry so far inside the official machine. The barest indication of what is done is given by the following quotation from the *Annual Review and Fixing of Farm Prices, 1951*:[1] 'National

[1] [8].

economic and budgetary considerations of a general character, the probable relative cost and availability of home and imported supplies and the physical capacity of the industry, bearing in mind the technical requirements of good husbandry, are all taken into account in deciding for each commodity what level of production is required in the national interest, as defined by Section 1 of the Agriculture Act, 1947.'

After looking forward to agricultural production in the future, the next step is an examination of the condition of the industry at present and in the immediate past. It is here that statistics play an important or even predominant part. Estimates are made independently by two different methods of the aggregate net income of agriculture for the current years ending on 31 May and in February. By net income is meant the difference between a farmer's receipts and expenses in the year, together with an appropriate addition or subtraction for changes in the value of farm stocks and work in hand during the year. The net income so derived has to provide the reward for the work of both the farmer and his wife together with a return on his capital, other than land. In the process of aggregation inter-farm transactions cancel out and the aggregate net income of the industry is equal to the net income of all agriculture, when treated as a single national farm. Apart from the two separate estimates of aggregate net income, which will be examined more minutely later on in this chapter, a body of statistics is also assembled giving detail of farm income and expenses for farms of different types and sizes situated in different parts of the country. On the Government side, these statistics are derived from material collected by agricultural economists at various universities, while the National Farmers' Union obtains independent figures under its own Farm Accounts Scheme.

Together with the estimates of aggregate net income, a further calculation is made of the aggregate amount of the increases in farmers' costs over the period since the last price review. Without anticipating the later discussion of the problems of estimation, it can be stated that the process of estimating the aggregate increases in cost is clearly much less hazardous than that of estimating the aggregate net income of the industry.

Before a start is made on the negotiations proper, all the statistical material mentioned so far is examined jointly by economists in the departments concerned and by representatives of the three Farmers' Unions. An attempt is then made to reach some common view about 'the general relevance and degree of reliability of the data'.[1] It is not clear what degree of agreement is usually attained at these meetings. There is some evidence, however, that the farmers' representatives tend to accept the year-to-year movements indicated by the official estimates,

[1] [8].

while denying, to some extent at any rate, the validity of the absolute figures. The official view, on the other hand, is that within limits reliance can be placed both on absolute figures for a given year and on the evidence about general trends.

Whatever the conclusions of this warming-up round of statistical bargaining, the full-scale negotiations between the official and farmers' representatives now start. The farmers are told of the Government's production objectives for the agricultural industry. The statistics are once more laid upon the table and an endeavour is made to reach a common interpretation of the evidence available concerning the general profitability of the industry. Naturally the negotiators' main concern is with the official estimates of aggregate net income, and their object is to agree within comparatively narrow limits on the necessary increase to be made in the farmer's aggregate net receipts if the production objectives are to be attained.

When a sufficient measure of agreement about the required overall adjustment has been reached, the two groups of representatives try to break down the figure so obtained into proposed changes in the prices of the individual 'review' commodities. Once comparatively close accord has been achieved on these prices, the official representatives report to their Ministers and the Government fixes the prices of the review products. During the whole process of the review, there is considerable interdepartmental activity interspersed between the meetings of the officials and the Farmers' Unions. In the event of wide differences of opinion the official representatives will have to ask their Ministers for further instructions, and negotiations may be prolonged for a month, or more.

Such in the barest outline is the machinery of the annual farm price review. In its operation the official estimates of aggregate net income are of extreme importance in influencing the results of the negotiations. It is, therefore, now necessary to analyse the way in which these estimates are obtained and to ask whether they are sufficiently robust to be a corner-stone of the Government's price-fixing policy.

THE NET INCOME STATISTICS

The Ministry of Agriculture makes two different estimates of the aggregate net income of agriculture for the current year. One of these is called the Departmental Net Income Calculation and the other is termed the Adjusted Raised Sample. The first-named is considered to be the more reliable, while the second is of the nature of a broad check on the first.

In the Departmental Net Income Calculation an estimate of the net income for the year ending 31 May is obtained by taking the difference between the net output of the industry, defined as the value of the gross output of agriculture at farm gate prices less the value of imports of feeding stuffs, store cattle, and seed, and the total expenses incurred by farmers during the period concerned. Net output on this definition is clearly not the same as the value added by British agriculture or net output on the Board of Trade's definition.

Net income obtained by this means is thus a residual estimate and will be markedly sensitive to relatively small proportional errors in the two totals that are subtracted from one another to obtain the answer. Consequently it is now necessary to consider the way in which the two estimates of aggregate net output and of total expense are built up. To make matters clear, Table 5 shows recent estimates.

On the output side it is helpful statistically that at present a very substantial part of the whole is subject to Governmental or other control. The Ministry of Food is intimately concerned with the production of

Table 5. *Details of 'Departmental' forecast of agricultural net income for 1950–1 and 1951–2*

	£ million				£ million	
	1950–1	1951–2			1950–1	1951–2
Farm expenses:			Sales:			
Labour	242½	255	Milk and milk products		299	301½
Rent and interest	58½	63	Fat stock		216	260½
Machinery expenses	115½	127½	Eggs and poultry		132½	144½
Feeding stuffs	139½	180	Farm crops		193½	196½
Fertilizers	54	59½	Horticultural products		91	112
Other expenses	126½	142	Other sales		18	28½
	736½	827			950	1,043½
Net income	293½	294	Subsidies, sundry receipts and other credits		35½	38½
			Increases in value of farm stocks and work in hand		44½	39
	1,030	1,121			1,030	1,121

Notes. (i) Owing to the one-large-farm character of the calculations, the figures for sales (£950 and £1,043½ million) exclude inter-farm transactions, and therefore do not represent the annual turnover of the industry.

(ii) The increases in value of farm stocks and work in hand (£44½ and £39 million) represent a component of net income which is not realized in cash during the year. Figures of £293½ and £294 million less £44½ and £39 million respectively (that is, £249 and £255 million) could be described as 'spendable net income', that is, available for living expenses, direct taxation, and financing necessary increases in capital.

(iii) The *latest* estimates of 'net income' for the years 1950–1 and 1951–2 are £262 million and £324½ million respectively.

Sources. Cmd. 8239, Cmd. 8556 and Cmd. 8798 [8]. The 1953 White Paper figures are not fully comparable.

cereals and livestock, while such commodities as hops and milk are disposed of through their respective Marketing Boards. Probably about four-fifths of agricultural gross output is subject to some sort of control, and this fact greatly facilitates the collection of statistical information. Even so there are likely to be discrepancies of varying sizes between the total disposals of these controlled commodities and the amounts that actually flow along the authorized channels. Part of the difference is of course accounted for by the quantities retained by farmers either for their personal consumption or for use as seed or feeding stuffs. But for such commodities as pigmeat there are likely to be significant quantities that are disposed of commercially and on which there is no direct statistical information.

In order to obtain estimates of the produce retained by farmers, some endeavour must be made to calculate total production of the various commodities. For crops this can be done using information about acreage and sample yields, but allowance must then be made for wastage in the process of harvesting and storage, and the appropriate correction may well vary widely according to the quality of the crops.[1]

These difficulties are magnified considerably in the attempts to estimate the gross output of those commodities for which there exists no system of controlled distribution, that is, broadly speaking, the horticultural group of agricultural products. Thus for fruit, vegetables, flowers and horticultural stock total production and total output (that is total production less wastage) can only be estimated using the information supplied by the Ministry of Agriculture's Local Horticultural Intelligence Committees. This information concerns the gross yields and the wastage of the various horticultural products grown in the Committees' areas, and can be used to build up the required totals from the acreages under various crops declared in the quarterly agricultural returns. The resulting estimates are clearly highly speculative and even figures of acreages are not as firm as they might first appear, since land may conceivably be cropped twice between successive agricultural returns.

But the process of estimation does not finish here, for in order to obtain figures for the value of output ex-farm prices must be applied to the output estimates. Once again the evidence as to the level of ex-farm prices is indirect, since the prices obtainable are wholesale market prices which must then be suitably adjusted for merchanting charges.

The estimates of the value both of sales and of total output of horticultural products are certainly the most vulnerable element in the estimate of net agricultural output, but it must be added that receipts

---

[1] For references to the official methods of crop estimation, see Britton and Hunt in Kendall [102].

from the sale of these products are only about 10 % of the total net farm receipts and are something under one-third of estimated net income. Thus, for example, an error of 5 % in the estimate of these sales would only introduce a $\frac{1}{2}$ % error into total net farm receipts and less than 2 % in aggregate net income.

Since estimated farm expenses relate to all work done on the farm, including expenditure on new drains and ditches, etc., which is really of a capital nature, a figure must be added to farmers' receipts to allow for this. Otherwise aggregate net income would be underestimated, as the implicit assumption would be made that all this work was a necessary expense in producing the current year's output.

An estimate must also be included among farmers' receipts of the value of the physical increase in stock and in work in progress. At present the treatment of different elements making up farmers' net investment in working capital during the year is not consistent. Thus only in the case of breeding stock does the value of net investment during the year represent the value of the physical (or real) increase; and for all other items of working capital the estimate used represents the change in the money value of work in progress rather than the value of the physical change. Some effort should clearly be made to tidy up this treatment. At present the definition of net income is a mixed one. It measures neither income after allowance has been made for maintaining physical capital intact nor yet income after preserving the money value of the capital. The income estimated is a hybrid concept somewhere between these two acceptable definitions.

Finally, on the receipts side of the farm account must be entered the total value of grants and subsidies received by farmers during the year. This figure clearly comes near to being a firm accounting figure and no comment upon its reliability is required.

If some of the estimates of the components of total receipts by farmers are somewhat shaky, at least the statistics can be obtained by the Ministry of Agriculture without a direct approach to the farmers themselves. On the expenditure side, the situation is not nearly so satisfactory in this particular respect. It is true that the Ministry of Agriculture obtain reliable information about wages by means of a sample inquiry conducted by their Wages Inspectors, and the information so obtained is used both for the annual price review and for wage enforcement.[1]

However, in the calculation of the total agricultural wages bill the Ministry is dependent on the details concerning numbers and categories of farm workers supplied by the farmers themselves. There is some evidence that farmers are not always sure how members of their own family who work on the farms should be classified. Thus the total

[1] See Palca and Davies, *Earnings and Conditions of Employment in Agriculture* [109].

expenditure on wages, which accounts for about one-third of all expenses, may well be subject to a significant degree of error.

It is unlikely that the estimates of payment of rent and interest can be very firmly based. A survey was carried out by the Central Landowners' Association[1] in conjunction with the Ministry of Agriculture and the Oxford University Agricultural Economics Research Institute, and the results were published in 1949 under the title of *The Rent of Agricultural Land in England and Wales, 1870–1946*. This investigation was more or less confined to the larger estates. There exists no comprehensive or up-to-date information about the current level of agricultural rents of all kinds.

As for interest, the Bankers' Association publish details of Bank Advances to Agriculture, but it is not clear that the figures may not also include advances made to activities ancillary to farming. Some estimate has also to be made of the amount of credit outstanding with merchants, and this can only be done by obtaining some idea of the total requirements of farmers in respect of working capital. In principle, the interest figure should include an allowance for the return on tenant's capital, but as no published recent estimate of this quantity exists it is difficult to see how such an allowance can be made in practice.

Since 1942 a census of agricultural machinery has been taken every two years, and the information obtained is used to provide an estimate for the annual amount spent on machinery repairs. In whatever manner such a calculation is carried out, there is little doubt that, in default of more direct evidence on actual expenditure, the results are somewhat conjectural.

Expenditure on feeding stuffs and fertilizers, which for the purposes of the net income calculation is equal to the value of imported feeding stuffs and fertilizers plus the merchanting and transport costs incurred in moving the home-produced varieties from farm to farm, can be fairly accurately found from trade or Government sources.

Enough has been said to show that if the receipts of the national farm are subject to a degree of uncertainty in their estimation, at least they are in total considerably more firmly based than the expenditure side, even if only because such a large proportion of agricultural output is controlled by a Government department at one stage or another.

It is scarcely necessary to emphasize once again that relatively small errors in the individual components of both expenses and receipts may well result in a substantial error in an estimate of net income which is obtained by difference between the sides of the account. It may well be that the various errors are of a random character, but some positive evidence of this fact must be adduced before much reliance can be

[1] Now County Landowners' Association.

placed on the chances of one error compensating another. During the process of statistical bargaining the farmers' representatives are likely to press the view that the official estimates of expenses are too low while those of the receipts items are too high, so that net income may eventually be subject to a downward bias, the extent of which depends on the pertinacity with which the farmers' case is presented. But even if an assumption of randomness is legitimate, this does not alter the fact that there is a great likelihood of a really large error in the residual estimate of aggregate net income.

What is available as a check upon the general reliability of the Departmental Net Income Calculation? The Provincial Agricultural Economists attached to universities in the United Kingdom collect accounts on a sample basis from round about 4,000 different farms. This inquiry was not designed to form a basis for any calculation of aggregate net income, but was intended to provide information for the study of farm management. It is not, therefore, surprising that figures thrown up by the Farm Management survey suffer from some very marked disadvantages when employed in a role for which they were never intended.

From the sampling point of view, there exists no adequate knowledge about the nature of the frame from which this sample of farms was drawn. This means that the process of 'raising' the sample to provide aggregate estimates is based upon premises which are either doubtful or known to be out of date. There is also considerable doubt about the randomness of the sample. The Provincial Agricultural Economists obtain their information by the voluntary co-operation of farmers. Unless some knowledge exists about the 'non-response' rate among different types and sizes of farms, there is no conceivable means by which any bias shown by the sample data can be corrected.

Sampling problems aside, the raised sample calculation uses different definitions and relates to a different time period from the Departmental Net Income Calculation. Thus in the farm accounts of the Farm Management survey the depreciation of machinery is taken as equal to the allowances granted for this purpose by the Board of Inland Revenue. The treatment of changes in livestock differs in the two calculations, while no attempt at all is made by the Provincial Agricultural Economists to value growing crops. The average farm year used ends in February and not on 31 May. This is particularly unfortunate as conspicuous changes may take place in the interval.

Finally, the information used is provided by the individual farmers themselves, and there can be little doubt that a regrettable but human upward bias is imparted to all expenses, while receipts declared are rather conservative estimates.

It is possible to attach rough orders of magnitude to the differences in the two estimates due to conceptual and timing variations. But such modifications seriously limit the use of the raised sample calculation as a check on the Departmental computation. The figure yielded by the raised sample cannot in all fairness be regarded as anything more than an estimate of the lower limit of aggregate net income. This conclusion is supported by the fact that, while the raised sample calculation produced a slightly higher figure for net income in 1937–8 and 1946–7 than the departmental estimate, in recent years the changes shown by the raised sample have been substantially and consistently smaller.

The strictures so far passed on the relative inadequacy and unreliability of the two calculations of aggregate net income, while severe, are not such as to indicate that the results are meaningless or that there is any very obvious way of improving the existing methods. But unfortunately a full picture has not been portrayed of the estimates that are deployed before the representatives of the Government and the farmers at the February price review. The earlier discussion was concerned with the difficulties of estimation once all the basic information had become available. But the price review takes place in February and an estimate is customarily produced of aggregate net income in the current year ending on 31 May, that is some three months later. Naturally it is not possible to collect details of farm accounts for the year which farmers have not yet completed. However, the Ministry of Agriculture has available the statistics that are required for its calculation for the first half of the current year. Thus it is that the figure obtained for the aggregate net income for the year about to end is in part an *estimate* as good (or as bad) as that for the previous year and in part a *forecast* based on an examination of existing trends and crude guesses about the effect of the existing and future weather.[1]

By projecting forward the experience of the first half of the year, and using general knowledge about current changes, a fairly good estimate can be made of the expenses that farmers will have met with during the whole year. Such an assertion cannot be repeated about the receipts side of the account, for here it is necessary to forecast agricultural output as a whole. In the spring many large and sudden alterations take place especially if the rate of output is tending to alter; and superimposed upon these farmer-activated changes is the further disturbing factor of the weather. It is not really pessimistic to suggest that in some years the forecasts of net income may differ from the later estimates by as much as 10 %. If such a large margin of error is indeed possible extreme caution is required in deducing the current profitability of the agricultural industry.

[1] The full details for a completed year are, for some odd reason, never published.

Nor is this the end of the story; the reward of the farmer is supposed to include an allowance for the vulnerability of his profits to changes in weather conditions. He must not be rewarded twice over for bearing these risks, nor must exceptionally favourable weather be allowed to rob him of an increase in prices justified by fast-rising costs. To avoid either pitfall, knowledge must be obtained of what the farmers would have received if the weather conditions had been in some sense 'normal' in the past and current years. Official observations on this adjustment ask that it 'be recognised...that only rough adjustments can be made for this purpose'[1] and indicate that it is based on known variations in the yields of crops, whether these be intended for sale or for feeding purposes. It must also take account of the variation in the condition of grazing land.

In principle little exception can be taken to the necessity of statistical modifications of this kind. The prospect, however, becomes most alarming when, after this final act of faith, the whole long chain of successive estimation is viewed in retrospect. How sensitive is the final result of such a cumulative process of computation, with wide possible margins of error at every stage? Does the whole business really make statistical sense? It is tempting to contrast the problem with that of calculating index numbers. Comparisons of price levels or of aggregate output over successive short periods are justifiable and indeed unavoidable, but can any meaning be attached to the claim that aggregate output has increased by so much over the last fifty years? With index numbers it is the gradual extension of the time period that causes doubts; with net agricultural income it is the long-drawn-out process of estimation, forecast and adjustment that is so frightening.

If these fears are taken seriously, it does not mean that the calculations should not be done. Rather it implies that while they must be done they should be looked at with extreme caution. The figures derived should be written on the backs of envelopes or pencilled upon the cuffs of the negotiators, but the firm and substantial appearance that they are given by being printed without extensive qualification in a Government White Paper should surely be avoided. This is not a plea that these extremely interesting and important estimates should not be published, but merely an expression of opinion that they should be presented so that even a layman can recognize them for what they are, that is, able and conscientious, but nevertheless highly speculative, attempts to answer extremely difficult questions.

[1] [8].

CALCULATING PRICES

However much the estimates purporting to give a general idea of the profitability of agriculture in the current year may be distrusted, it is fair to remark that forecasts of aggregate cost[1] increases, arising from decisions already taken since the last price review and falling to be borne in the following year, can be fairly well assessed; though they must depend on forecasts about numbers employed and imported materials used. Thus if it is accepted that farmers have obtained a fair return for their endeavours in the current year, a strong case can be pressed for increasing the general level of prices of the review products so as to reimburse them for these increases in expenses in the ensuing year.

But to know within narrow limits the extent of the rise in expenses is one thing, and the calculation of an adequate recompense is another. If a global addition is made to farm receipts precisely equal to the aggregate increase in expenses, this means that the farmers retain the whole benefit accruing from increases in productivity due either to improvements in technique or to the increased amount of capital per farm. The policy of assured markets and annual price fixing has raised agriculture from the status of a depressed industry to one of an industry receiving treatment no less favourable than any other economic activity. The community at large cannot fairly be asked to deny itself all participation in the benefits of a more efficient and productive agriculture. Thus before aggregate increases in expenses can be translated into increased receipts for farmers, some estimate ought to be made of the increase in productivity to be expected during the year. It would then be necessary to apportion the benefits of such a rise between the farming population, including labourers, and the community at large. There is no evidence that such a division is accepted either in principle or in practice at present.

Once the aggregate increase in farmers' receipts sufficient to give a reasonable reward at the level of costs appropriate to the next year has been determined, there comes the scarcely less intricate problem of allocating this global sum to price increases (or falls) of the various review commodities. It is here that the concept of a national farm reveals its limitations. The Government and the populace at large may feel that there is justice in raising substantially the price of one product and compensating such an increase by lowering (or not raising as much) the prices of others, if the national interest appears to demand that the existing balance of agricultural production be substantially altered. The specialist producers of the highly favoured review product may find

---

[1] These should more properly be called increases in 'expenses', but 'cost' is the official term.

little cause for complaint. Farmers who can fairly easily change over from the output with the lower prices to that with the increased prices will reflect that alterations in the profitability of roundabouts and swings are more or less self-compensating. But producers who must perforce concentrate upon producing the least rewarded review products will not accept the proposed change without violent protests. The specialist dairy farmers will exert themselves to the full to resist a fall in the price of milk, say, which from the point of view of the national farm is to be offset by a rise in the price of wheat.

This clash of interests within the farm community as a whole cannot be expected to redound to the advantage of the Government negotiators. In so far as the aggrieved section organizes a pressure group, while the remainder are passive and complacent, the Government will be faced with a demand for all prices to be increased to cover increased expenses, and the desired shift of production will merely require that some prices are raised more than others. This tendency for all prices to increase at least as much as costs was not such a serious embarrassment so long as there remained a cushion of some £400 million between expenditure by consumers and receipts paid to farmers. But as internal inflationary pressure has been curbed and the food subsidies substantially diminished, then demand and not only cost of production has begun to play its part in price formation.

Information on the relative profitability of different kinds of farming is provided both by the Farm Management Survey and the National Farmers' Union Farm Accounts Scheme. Comparison between the two sets of data is difficult because of the different classifications used, but there do not appear to be any violent contradictions between them. Neither sample can be truly regarded as unbiased from a statistical point of view, and the extent of the bias so far remains undetermined. Both investigations determine the relative profitability of different types of farms in different areas from the tax collector's point of view rather than from that of an economist.

POSSIBILITIES OF IMPROVEMENT

What proposals for improvement emerge from this brief examination of existing statistical practice at agricultural price reviews? Some people may feel that too much is being attempted on inadequate information and that the free play of market forces operating within a framework of suitable safeguards might produce results that were no more arbitrary and just as satisfactory. An examination of the justification of such a claim is outside the terms of reference of the present investigation. Here it is required to ask whether what is being done could be done better and not whether it should be done at all.

Within this more restricted sphere of discussion, it does not seem that the difficulties of consistent definition or of estimation are the most conspicuous features of the present practice. The most marked impression is that of the general lack of statistical design and of the prolonged application of a method which was hastily devised *ad hoc* to deal with a sudden problem. This method, although no doubt subjected to continual refinements, would seem to be capable of substantial improvement without necessarily requiring the employment of increased statistical manpower. The integration and co-ordination of the at present independent investigations would seem to promise a substantial increase in reliability.

Why should not a single annual sample survey of farms be conducted under the joint auspices of the Ministry of Agriculture (and its counterpart in Northern Ireland and Scotland), the Provincial Agricultural Economists and the various National Farmers' Unions? This inquiry could be designed to yield directly all the information required by each of three collaborating bodies. Thus the activities of the Agricultural Economists, the Ministry's wage inspectors and the National Farmers' Union Accountants could be made to support and complement each other instead of merely providing a vague and inadequate cross-check.

It may be that sufficiently up-to-date information on which to base a thoroughly satisfactory sample survey does not at present exist. If so, then there is a case for conducting a new National Farm Survey similar to that undertaken in the years 1941–3.[1]

The sample selected would not necessarily have to be of enormous size to secure the requisite degree of reliability. The employment of the devices of multi-stage sampling, that is selecting at random first large areas, then perhaps smaller areas at random from within the larger areas and finally farms from within the smaller areas, and of stratification, that is the inclusion of a relatively high number of those types of farm the experience of which was known to be highly variable and a comparatively small number of the sorts of farm which had fairly standardized experience, would ensure a significant economy of effort. Provided that the National Farmers' Unions gave the annual survey their blessing, information on matters other than wages might well be collected on a voluntary basis. A certain number of farmers refusing to co-operate would not necessarily impair the random nature of the sample provided that some knowledge was obtained about the characteristics of the farms excluded for this reason.

While it would probably be desirable that at least a part of the sample was chosen afresh each year, each year's sample could contain a standing subsample the composition of which did not vary from year to year.

The difficulties of obtaining agreement over a commonly acceptable

[1] See *National Farm Survey of England and Wales, a summary report* [68].

set of definitions should be capable of resolution. All parties concerned would not have to agree on what is properly to be regarded as a farmer's net income, but sufficient information would have to be elicited so that all reasonable varieties of net income could be calculated.

The question arises at what time of year such a survey could be carried out. It is certainly necessary that a farmer should only be asked to provide such information at a relatively slack period of his year. Also the information obtained must be sifted and digested in time for the annual price review in February. This would mean that the survey would have to take place in December and should provide information about the second half of the previous farming year, that is December to May (inclusive), and for the first half of the current year, that is June to November (inclusive). These dates would not, unfortunately, tie in very well with existing farm accounting practice, since most accounting years end in March and April although there are significant numbers that finish in September, October and December.

Such a time-table is a fairly tight one and may well necessitate some modifications of accounting practice. Even if it can be adhered to, no more information will be available about the second half of the current farming year than before, if survey information is restricted to the past. But there is no reason why the members of the sample should not be asked in broad terms about their intentions during the period December to May. Such knowledge would be considerably more valuable than extrapolation based on hunches or apparent past trends.

A comprehensive annual survey of this type, quite apart from improving the estimates and forecasts of aggregate net income, would enable the distribution of net income by individual farms of various types and sizes to be estimated. Whether such knowledge would enable the price-fixing process to be carried out more smoothly is perhaps open to doubt; but at least difficulties arising from a clash of interests within the agricultural community might be more clearly foreseen.[1]

The suggested integration of statistical effort, if achieved, would not render the data used for the Departmental Net Income Calculation superfluous or useless. The various global figures would contine to be of the utmost importance. The firmly based component estimates of various items of receipts and of expenditure could be used as controls for the information thrown up by the sample survey. Thus it would be possible to estimate and correct for the apparent amount of over- and under-reporting in the returns of individual farmers. This practice of tying up aggregate indirect estimates with sample survey information has been used with great advantage in various investigations in the United States.[2] Rather than there being a conflict between the technique

[1] See p. 77 above.   [2] See *Studies in Income and Wealth* [**108**].

of aggregate indirect estimation and the blowing up of sample data, the firmer estimates of one method can be used to strengthen the weaker elements of the other. Indeed, unless something of this kind is done the best possible sampling procedure will remain ineffective in the face of deliberate misstatement by, or the short memories of, human beings.

From an altogether different standpoint, the heavy reliance at present placed on the Departmental Net Income Calculation is to be regretted. That the estimates of aggregate net receipts are as good as they are is in very large measure attributable to the extensive character of existing Governmental controls. If such control is substantially diminished in the future, the statistical fabric of the present policy would be severely damaged. This sort of disaster would be avoided, or reduced considerably in magnitude, if the necessary statistics were not so indissolubly wedded to current administrative practice. By all means let the Government statisticians make full use of the facts that day-to-day administration throws up, but do not let them expose themselves to the risk that administrative changes will deprive them totally of vital information.

A gradual shift of emphasis from the old methods of making use of existing information, however bad, because no one will provide what is really wanted, to a full exploitation of the potentialities of direct approaches to farmers on a sample basis, would provide valuable indications of the possibilities and limitations of the new methods. As increased experience was obtained, firmer reliance could progressively be placed on the sample survey data. When and if the old methods were no longer applicable, the statisticians and administrators would know precisely how much faith they could have in information given by the annual sample and what independent global cross-checks were vital. They would not be overtaken by the march of events and forced yet again to make *ad hoc* improvisations, which, however justifiable in wartime, are certainly unsatisfactory after eight years or so of near-peace.

The statistics used for agricultural price-fixing are clearly directly involved in policy determination; there is none of the tenuous and doubtful connexion which we have noted in previous chapters. Our discussion shows the need for proper design in obtaining figures on which so much weight is to be placed; and it can be seen also that a careful examination of their possible errors (and the interrelation of their errors) is vital. The suggestions we have made may not be sufficiently detailed or practical to be constructive; but when the general ideas which they contain have been seriously explored by all the interested parties, it would surely be possible to overcome the practical difficulties.

CHAPTER VIII

THE BALANCE OF EXTERNAL PAYMENTS

The following words from an official publication make a suitable introduction to the subject of this chapter: 'The purpose of a balance of payments is to summarise and analyse a country's financial and economic transactions with the outside world. The results of such an analysis show how far the country is living within its "current" overseas income, and whether it is borrowing or investing overseas. But the analysis has significance for other purposes: in elucidating the reasons for external payments difficulties, and the results of actions taken to combat them; for the planning of financial and commercial policy; in illustrating the magnitude and pattern of the international exchange of goods and services; and for the compilation of estimates of the national income.'[1] The United States view is that 'the statement fulfils the dual purpose of reflecting all international economic transactions of a country while at the same time exhibiting the net effect of these transactions on the nation's financial position.'[2]

These quotations relate to the published balance-of-payments statistics, which are described in more detail below; but these are but a summary, in a sense a by-product, of the wide range of facts which have to be collected to help to determine external financial policy and to illuminate its effects. This, for those outside the Treasury, is a very difficult and complex field. A distinction has to be made between the accounts of the external receipts and payments of the United Kingdom— which is the important unit when one is thinking of the immediate results of internal policy—and the accounts of the whole sterling area, which show the calls made on the central reserve of gold and dollars. A full understanding of the external financial relations of the sterling area requires in effect the study of the balances of payments of a number of countries which employ differing methods and may classify their data in different ways. An understanding of the 'strength or weakness of sterling' may indeed require more than this—nothing less than a study of the world-wide uses of sterling as an international currency. Once one leaves the (relatively) solid ground of visible trade statistics, one meets the mists of secrecy which necessarily shroud much of the workings of exchange control, and which conceal the relations of bankers to their customers. What the outsider can know is very largely what the Treasury

[1] *United Kingdom Balance of Payments, 1946–50* [**11a**].
[2] *The Balance of International Payments of the United States, 1946–1948* [**72**].

chooses to release to him, and it will necessarily be a brief selection from the processed result of all the official statistical activity. It does not lie in the power of the British authorities to reveal information about the sterling area position which they obtain in confidence from other Governments; and London's world banking business would hardly be encouraged if the transactions of its customers were published, except in a very much consolidated form.

On the other hand it would be exceedingly unfortunate if Government action relating to external finance were to be, like military policy, largely immune from criticism because no outsider can have access to the secret information on which it is based. The power to conceal facts necessary to a decision is one which should very rarely be given to public servants. It is therefore in the public interest that the Treasury and the Bank of England should publish, not only as many facts as possible, but also as much information as they can about how the figures are obtained and what errors they may contain. Intelligent study of the statistics is only possible if the firm figures can be distinguished from the guesses and the balancing items. Furthermore, it is not desirable that the information should be published in a form so highly technical and compressed that it is accessible only to a handful of experienced economic statisticians.

We shall be making a general examination of these important principles in Chapters x and xi. It is convenient to begin our study of the balance-of-payments statistics with what is published, before attempting to go behind the scenes to look at the adequacy of the whole body of information for the needs of the policy-makers. It is not possible to go here into all the complexities of the subject, and the reader is referred to two helpful articles: 'The Oversea Trade Statistics of the United Kingdom', by A. Maizels,[1] and 'Statistics of the Balance of Payments', by Professor R. G. D. Allen.[2]

THE WHITE PAPER AND ITS SOURCES

In the revised series of half-yearly White Papers, which started in October 1950, the amounts recorded are transactions, rather than payments or receipts; thus the United Kingdom is taken to owe country X £y million the moment a consignment of goods to this value passes into U.K. ownership. This procedure was a change from previous practice, and (in this particular respect, and in principle) brought the balance-of-payments estimates into line with the national income estimates.

Since this change took place the presentation of the balance-of-payments estimates has remained virtually unaltered up to the present

---

[1] Maizels in Kendall [102].   [2] [86].

time (1953). In Part I of the White Paper there is a summary table showing the main items of the United Kingdom's general balance of payments for a short series of years, distinguishing a Current Account and an Investment and Financing Account. This table is followed by others giving in summary the United Kingdom's regional balances of payments for the same period of years.

Part II shows in greater detail the interrelationship between the United Kingdom's balances of payments with each of the main regions, for each year separately.[1] The capital (or Investment and Financing) account is, in these tables, considerably elaborated. The capital transactions with each of the regions are enumerated under five main headings—'grants, etc.'; 'gold, sterling and other transfers, etc.'; 'overseas investment, borrowing, etc.'; 'U.K. sterling liabilities, etc.'; and changes in gold and dollar reserves. The etceteras bear silent witness to the necessary roughness of any such classification. Each of the headings, except the last, is further subdivided.

Special aspects of the balance of payments are presented in Part III. Attention is first directed at the sterling area's gold and dollar accounts. The current and capital account transactions of the United Kingdom with the dollar area are again set out, and also both the net transactions of the rest of the sterling area with the dollar area, and the other net transactions of the whole sterling area involving gold and dollars. The total of this table is the net gold and dollar surplus or deficit, and another shows in detail (by quarters) how this surplus or deficit was financed. Further tables analyse in similar detail the net surplus or deficit of the United Kingdom in the European Payments Union.

Part IV deals with reserves and liabilities; the quarterly movements of the sterling area's gold and dollar reserves, the U.K. sterling liabilities, the official holdings of non-dollar currencies, and the credit or debit balance of the United Kingdom with E.P.U. Then follows Part V, the *explanatory notes to tables*, which now include a table reconciling the figures of U.K. imports and exports in the *Trade and Navigation Accounts* with those in the White Paper itself. The notes also give extra details of the visible trade of the 'Rest of the Sterling Area' with the dollar area, details of special receipts by the United Kingdom from the United States, and some additional data on 'Rest of Sterling Area' transactions with O.E.E.C. countries.

The impressive array of figures contained in this slim official paper cannot be assembled from raw data accessible elsewhere. Much reliance has to be placed on the statistics thrown up in the administration of exchange control by the Bank of England. Other information is

[1] The regions are: the dollar area: 'other Western hemisphere'; O.E.E.C. countries; other non-sterling countries; the rest of the sterling area; and the non-territorial organizations.

obtained by an exchange of information with our trading partners in the sterling area. The information on U.K. visible trade contained in the monthly *Trade and Navigation Accounts* has, as we shall see, to be processed and adapted. The result of this construction from varied types of information is that there is a good deal of difference in the reliability of the figures. Thus, statistics of the payments made for imports are on the whole more reliable than those of receipts from exports; and the 'controlled' capital transactions with the non-sterling world can be estimated more reliably than the transactions with the rest of the sterling area.

The White Paper gives only brief indications of the sources which it employs, though it gives extensive details about coverage. The visible imports from the non-sterling world are recorded, partly by the purchasing departments of the Government, and partly when the transactions pass through the exchange control mechanism of the Bank of England (which passes information to the Overseas Finance Division of the Treasury). For imports from the rest of the sterling area the *Trade and Navigation Accounts* must be used, adjusted for timing and coverage, and supplemented on occasion by the trade statistics of the members of the sterling area involved. The statistics of imports in the *Trade and Navigation Accounts* relate to the physical movement of goods into the ports of the United Kingdom. In fact the ownership of goods intended for importation usually vests in the United Kingdom or its citizens at or before the time of shipment from the country of origin. The Trade Accounts coverage is not wholly appropriate for balance-of-payments purposes with respect either to areas[1] or to commodities.[2] Furthermore, the Trade Accounts value imports on a c.i.f.[3] basis, while for the balance of payments it is necessary to account separately for the transport and insurance services rendered by other countries; a payment for a service of this kind rendered by a British company is clearly not an international transaction.

The difficulties of estimating the transactions in visible exports are similar or worse. Once again the Trade Accounts provide the raw data, but in this case for trade with non-sterling as well as with sterling countries. There is no difficulty about valuation, since the Trade Accounts value exports f.o.b. (free on board, that is as they are placed on the ship). But the ownership of U.K. exports is believed usually to change on or after arrival in foreign ports, and thus a 'lag' must be

---

[1] The White Paper excludes imports from and exports to the Channel Islands, and landings by British whale fisheries.

[2] [11b], p. 31; see also Maizels [102] and Allen [86]. The recent decision to revise the classification of the Trade Accounts will bring a valuable increase in their usefulness.

[3] Cost, insurance, freight.

allowed for the change in ownership if the Trade Accounts figures are to be made to correspond with the White Paper definitions.

The estimation of this lag may require enquiries to be made of the exporters of different kinds of goods, or some rough determination of the probable time of the goods in transit between the United Kingdom and the country of consignment. But to assume the lag constant, though it may not result in serious error taking one year with another, will lead to misleading conclusions if at any time speculation for or against the pound takes the form of speeding up or delaying payments. Such a change could not be measured, since there would not be, at least under present circumstances, enough information about the corresponding changes in short-term credit. It appears from the White Paper that such parts of the change as do not already affect the figures from exchange control would be included in the balancing item in the Investment and Financing Account.

For invisible items, information is not nearly so complete as for visible trade, even on the import side of the account. Firms such as oil, insurance and shipping companies are allowed by the exchange control to carry a 'float' of dollars, and to render an account of their transactions at stated periods. Government transactions appear on both sides of the account, and are presumably firm figures. But for some sections of invisible exports estimates made by private bodies have to be used—for example for shipping receipts and the earnings from 'tourism'. Thus in 1947 the Chamber of Shipping carried out at the request of the Government an investigation into the contribution of the United Kingdom's shipping to the country's invisible exports;[1] for more recent years some of the figures required have had to be built up on the foundation provided by this study.

We have mentioned earlier that the balance-of-payments statisticians do not rely wholly on home-produced information. Frequently a friendly interchange of knowledge enables a very rough estimate to be replaced by a firmer figure obtained from foreign or commonwealth sources.[2] This practice might before now have been extended with advantage to all concerned, but for the international differences in methods of valuation and in the classification of trade[3] and the lack of knowledge about the time lags or leads involved.

---

[1] Kendall, 'The U.K. Mercantile Marine and its Contribution to the Balance of Payments' [101].

[2] Tourist expenditure in the Republic of Ireland is one example; earnings from colonial plantations are another.

[3] For details of some of these differences see Maizels [102]. Considerable progress has been made, both before the Second World War by the League of Nations, and more recently by the United Nations and O.E.E.C., in securing the wider adoption of an internationally agreed system of classification.

The great detail shown in the capital, or Investment and Financing, account is almost entirely due to the statistics derived from the operation of exchange control. The U.S. balance-of-payments statisticians are understood to envy the fine breakdown of transactions which we can achieve under the broad heading of Inter-Area Transfers.[1] But the picture is somewhat marred by the existence of a heterogeneous item entitled 'Other capital transactions (net)' which falls under the main heading of 'Overseas investment, borrowing, etc.' This important item requires a long footnote to explain it, which is reproduced here practically in full:

'This is a miscellaneous item. Sales and redemptions of sterling area securities and sales of direct investments in the sterling area are included together with an estimate of movements of funds between the United Kingdom and the Rest of the Sterling Area (including those for commercial investment). It also includes minor adjustments in the sterling value of the Exchange Equalisation Account's holdings of foreign currencies due to changes in exchange rates [but excluding the change due to sterling devaluation in 1949].

'The item also contains the "balancing item" involved in the construction of a complete balance of payments with the whole world. The inadequacy of data on long and short-term capital movements is an important factor leading to this balancing item; another factor is the variation in commercial credit. The inclusion of this balancing item in Section III of the Investment and Financing Account should not be taken to imply that full agreement between this Account and the Current Account has been achieved by independent estimation of each, but only that there is a strong presumption that the greater part of the residual is of a capital nature. A part of this balancing item arises in connection with, and is included in, the regional balances of payments with the Dollar Area, Other Western Hemisphere and O.E.E.C. countries; the remainder is attributed to the Rest of the Sterling Area, between which and the United Kingdom capital movements are especially difficult to identify; no part of it is attributed... to Other non-sterling countries. For that area the major uncertainty arises in connection with its balance with the Rest of the Sterling Area rather than from unrecorded capital transactions with the United Kingdom.'[2]

One unfortunate feature here is the absence of information about variations in commercial credit, since these may play a crucial part in short-run balance-of-payments difficulties. The information at the

[1] This is the heading used in Part I of the White Paper. In Part II the more extensive title of 'Gold, Sterling and other transfers, etc.' appears. The transactions concerned are those involving a change in the regional distribution of United Kingdom indebtedness, but no alteration in its absolute size.

[2] [11b].

disposal of the Board of Trade through its export credit guarantees business covers too narrow a section of the field to be of practical use. Broadly speaking, the 'unidentified flow' is a combination of cumulated errors and omissions in all other items of the accounts, of unknown receipts from abroad, and of leakages to overseas—either legally, through variations in credit, or through illegal transactions anywhere in the sterling area.

In both current and capital accounts the official statisticians show 'net entries'.[1] This does not necessarily mean that the information necessary to split such an item into its component money flows is not available, although in particular instances, for example 'other capital transactions (net)', this may be true. It may be necessary to resort to such devices to preserve confidentiality,[2] or because the net estimate is more reliable than any of the bits into which it might be broken. The White Paper does not in fact distinguish, except by an occasional hint (for example in the note quoted on p. 84 above), between the reliabilities of the many estimates that it contains. Presumably some undeclared convention has been adopted about the maximum degree of unreliability to be tolerated in a printed figure.

THE WHITE PAPER AND THE PUBLIC

Before we come to make some surmises about the adequacy of the statistical help given to those who determine policy, it will be convenient to consider whether the White Paper does its duty as a published document—that of conveying information to the right people, in a form which is useful to them. It is perhaps a little ungracious to complain of any shortcomings, for there is no doubt that the information now given is a great addition to statistical resources. Nevertheless, in some ways the White Paper falls between two stools; it is not just what the expert wants, nor is it an effective means of conveying information to the layman.

The expert, if he is to have a really careful and scholarly understanding of the forces at work on the balance of payments, would of course like more information. There are probably good reasons why not much more can be published, but it is difficult to believe that the limits of publication have yet been reached. The behaviour of the 'balancing item', for instance, is of great importance; the 1953 White Papers give, in a footnote, a little information about it (as distinct from the 'known' capital transfers with which it is amalgamated in the tables). But this

---

[1] That is, entries on one side of an account only, representing the difference between flows of transactions in opposite directions.

[2] For example for oil companies, or for information provided from overseas which the United Kingdom is not free to publish in detail.

information is rounded to the nearest £50 million or £100 million; there is no obvious reason why the balancing item should not be shown separately, at its correct figure, in accordance with the practice adopted by the United States statisticians.

The expert, even if he can be allowed no more figures, can properly expect some discussion of the methods used to obtain them. Ideally this discussion would include an assessment of errors; and, despite the serious practical or political difficulties of an open admission of errors, we think that it would be possible and healthy to attempt some such discussion in a technical paper. But a description, however broad and general, of methods would go a long way to enable the expert to use the figures with understanding. What is needed is a more elaborate and detailed annual analysis aimed at the technical experts; and, if it is objected that they are so few that it is not worth while to take so much trouble on their behalf, it must be remembered that the exercise of describing what they have done would be a valuable help to the official statisticians, and the final result would have many uses within the Treasury and the Bank.

But such an annual publication would not be enough. It is to the advantage of Britain that those who (in any part of the world) comment on her external position should do so with understanding, and should not draw irrelevant conclusions from such things as changes in gold reserves or in E.P.U. balances. The present White Paper provides nourishment only for the specialist, and it is supplemented only by the unsatisfactory annual discussion in the *Economic Survey*. There would be a most useful place for the descriptive article, aimed at an intermediate public, such as appears in the pages of the U.S. *Survey of Current Business*. Such articles, which might ultimately be quarterly rather than half-yearly, could include the latest figures necessary to bring up to date the story as shown in the regular publications.

THE NEEDS OF POLICY

The White Paper, as we have remarked above, is a by-product of a larger activity required to illuminate the effects of policy and help to decide its changes. While it is valuable to explain what has happened in the past—if only in order to avoid repeating errors in the future—the policies actually determined have to fit into a pattern of expected events in the future. What one would like to have, ideally, is a forecast of the balance of payments—not just for the United Kingdom, but for the whole sterling area as well. Indeed, what is needed in theory is a series of forecasts, corresponding to the different combinations of policy which Britain and the members of the Commonwealth might pursue, and to different expectations about the course of prices, supplies and so forth.

In fact, of course, so complicated a framework could not be erected, and it would be about as much use as the Tower of Babel if it were. Policy has to be determined by a process of broad judgement, which statistics can assist by eliminating what is obviously unwise and suggesting the likely magnitudes of the effects of policy changes. Obviously the greatest help will be given by those statistics which can be obtained quickly for recent periods of time; and these are thrown up in good measure by the operation of exchange control, by the Trade Accounts, by the returns of the gold and dollar reserves and of E.P.U., and so forth. There is a useful analogy between the whole process and the technique of navigation. The first stage is to take observations; then one calculates the present position and direction of movement; finally one consults the charts and the weather forecasts to see what rocks, submerged obstacles or squalls are in the vicinity. But when all this is done, navigation depends partly on dead reckoning and partly on the direct observation of a few isolated landmarks.

It is possible that the Treasury and the Bank have not yet equipped themselves with quite all the instruments which safe navigation demands. It is noticeable that the statistics which are known to be used are mostly thrown up as a by-product of administration. There may be a place for the wider use of specially designed sample surveys, both to fill gaps and to provide a check on the accuracy of information already used. Tourist expenditure and shipping receipts are possible fields for this. Many more such special inquiries would be needed if the great flow of information which at present comes from exchange control were to cease. It may be that some control over capital movements will continue indefinitely; but it might be administratively very different from that at present operated, and fail to throw up the range of information at present used. Some time would be needed to develop and test alternative statistical instruments, and it is to be hoped that they are already being planned.

It is not certain how far the authorities are equipped with the statistical equivalent of radar—that is to say, with means of giving advance warning of obstacles. Presumably use is made of information about outstanding export orders and of the warnings given by changes in stocks. The considerable reduction in the area of Government trading may, however, mean that more elaborate information systems will be needed in the future. But there is no point in elaborating information until it is so complicated that it cannot be used; and it is very difficult to judge the right division of effort between making guesses about the future and learning the lessons of the past. If one cannot see far ahead, then the safest thing may be to concentrate on making the craft manœuvrable—that is, to devise instruments of policy which can make small changes of direction quickly.

AMERICAN PRACTICE

What can we learn by looking at the practice of the United States in dealing with its balance-of-payments statistics? It is well to start by emphasizing the great difference in environment. The United States has no real balance-of-payments worries; it is not a guardian of the inadequate reserves of a collection of countries (as Britain is for the sterling area); it does not have to trouble about inconvertibility or exchange control. Thus for the U.S. statisticians the construction of a balance of payments is more of an academic exercise, not thrown up as a by-product of urgent policy decisions.

Many of the data have to be collected by specially conducted sample investigations. Fortunately (and in part because of the wise and helpful policy of the statisticians) the attitude of the public and of banks and businesses is not opposed to the provision of the information. The idea that a knowledge of one's past operations will somehow be to the advantage of one's competitors does not command the support that it gets in the United Kingdom.

While individual estimates in the U.S. balance of payments are often considerably less reliable than the corresponding British figures, there is probably a rather wider coverage of the whole field of transactions. The current account and the capital account can be estimated separately and a residual estimate of the discrepancy due to errors and omissions obtained. This item is not random over time, but appears to be significantly associated with movements of short-term indebtedness. It is usually larger (in relation to turnover) than the balancing item in the U.K. White Paper, and this is an indication of the greater efficiency of estimation from exchange control data.

The balance-of-payments estimates are compiled by the Department of Commerce and published every quarter in the *Survey of Current Business*, with a lapse of about two months after the period to which they refer. At irregular intervals the department publishes a substantial pamphlet analysing in great detail, and with the help of many tables and charts, the changes in the various items of the balance of payments over a period of years.[1] These descriptive works also contain appendices on the concepts and definitions used and on the methodology and sources of data for the whole statistical exercise. Both the pamphlets and the explanatory articles in the *Survey of Current Business* describe the broad movements in non-technical language.

As we have already suggested, Britain has something to learn from the United States in the matter of presentation; and U.S. experience

---

[1] See, for example, [72].

should also be of great value in devising techniques for replacing information lost through changes in exchange control.

THE INTERNATIONAL MONETARY FUND PROPOSALS

In an endeavour to obtain balance-of-payments statistics for many countries on a standard basis, the International Monetary Fund has laid down a prescribed form of current and capital accounts. This includes a fine breakdown of transactions, and also asks for a reconciliation of export and import values on Trade Account and balance-of-payments definitions. The latter was provided in part by the 1953 White Paper [11 b]. The Fund's standard form, from its instructions to its member countries, is reproduced overleaf.[1]

At present the United Kingdom can provide more or less all that is required in the current account, but makes a pretty poor showing in the capital account. This is not, however, necessarily an adverse comment on the British balance of payments. The statisticians concerned have tended to adopt a 'practical' outlook; the International Monetary Fund's economists and statisticians, on the other hand, have a more 'intellectual' approach. While they should be given full credit for their work in standardizing and clarifying balance-of-payments receipts they do seem to demand, as a matter of course, information which even countries with highly developed statistical services find extremely difficult to provide, and it may be that they fail to perceive the full implications of requiring the submission of very finely detailed statements. If aggregates of transactions estimated with a reasonable degree of reliability have to be broken down into subdivisions to an excessive degree, the figures quoted must often be suspected of having a wide margin of error. Yet the Fund has prescribed no way of indicating the relative degree or the associations of the errors in various transactions and subtotals of transactions. On this problem Professor Allen writes:

'The question is how to show the uncertain components. Two cases can be distinguished. First, a number of items may be thrown together into an aggregate. This may be because only rough estimates are available for them separately and aggregation is done in the hope that errors will offset each other. Or it may be because the sources of information provide a broad total but not the components which cannot be identified except on an incomplete or sample basis. Secondly, there must be a residual, or balancing item. If all important items are separately estimated, the residual is a simple allowance for "errors and omissions". More usually, one or more items are not capable of separate estimation and the residual covers them, together with "errors and omissions" from the rest of the account.

[1] *Balance of Payments Manual* [79].

STANDARD SCHEDULE FOR REPORTING

A. *Current transactions*

Reporting country..................   Period covered ....

Currency .... Unit ....   Exchange rate, U.S. $.........per............

Item	Credit (receipts)	Debit (payments)	Net credit or debit (−)
1. Merchandise (1·1 plus 1·2)			
1·1. Exports and imports (both f.o.b.)			
1·2. Other			
2. Non-monetary gold movement (net) ...			
3. Foreign travel			
4. Transportation (4·1 plus 4·2)			
4·1. Gross freight			
4·2. Other			
5. Insurance			
6. Investment income (6·1 through 6·3) ...			
6·1. Direct investment			
6·2. Other interest			
6·3. Other equity			
7. Government, not included elsewhere (7·1 plus 7·2)			
7·1. Military expenditure and surplus property			
7·2. Other			
8. Miscellaneous			
Total goods and services (1 through 8)...			
9. Donations (9·1 through 9·4)			
9·1. Personal and institutional remittances			
9·2. Other private transfers			
9·3. Reparations			
9·4. Official grants			
10. Total current transactions (1 through 9)			
ERRORS AND OMISSIONS (16 minus 10)	......	......	

(Reproduced from p. 26 of the *Balance of Payments Yearbook* [79].)

BALANCE OF PAYMENTS TO FUND

B. *Movement of capital and monetary gold*

Reporting country................   Period covered ....
Currency ....   Unit........   Exchange rate, U.S. $.........per............

Item	Net movement increasing (+) or decreasing (−)		
	Assets	Liabilities	Net assets
PRIVATE (excluding banking institutions)			
11. Long-term capital (11·1 through 11·6)			
11·1. Direct investment			
11·2. Portfolio securities: bonds ...			
11·3. Portfolio securities: shares			
11·4. Amortization			
11·5. Other contractual repayments			
11·6. Other			
12. Short-term capital (12·1 plus 12·2) ...			
12·1. Currency, deposits, Government obligations		......	
12·2. Other			
OFFICIAL AND BANKING INSTITUTIONS			
13. Long-term capital (13·1 through 13·6)			
13·1. Official loans			
13·2. Bank loans			
13·3. Portfolio securities			
13·4. Amortization			
13·5. Other contractual repayments			
13·6. Other			
14. Short-term capital (14·1 through 14·4)			
14·1. Payments and clearing agreements			
14·2. Liabilities to I.M.F. and I.B.R.D.	......		
14·3. Other liabilities to official and banking institutions	......		
14·4. Other			
15. Monetary gold		......	
16. Total movement of capital and monetary gold (11 through 15)			

(Reproduced from p. 27 of the *Balance of Payments Yearbook* [79].)

'To insist upon subdivision of aggregates of these kinds is calculated to retard rather than to assist the development of balance-of-payments accounts.'[1]

It is probable that Professor Allen's words sum up the British point of view, to which reference has already been made. If it is assumed that no noticeable modification is made in either the International Monetary Fund's or the British method of presenting balance-of-payments statistics, then it is hard to refute the logic of his arguments. But if an official effort were made both to allocate subjective margins of error to individual estimates and to indicate the degree of association between the errors in pairs of entries, the objections that Professor Allen puts forward would be largely met.

As the International Monetary Fund's standard form for balance-of-payments statistics has been mentioned in the past discussion it is perhaps worth while to refer to the concept of 'compensatory official financing'. Roughly speaking, this category of transactions refers to those undertaken especially by Governments to finance that part of the deficit on current account not financed by more normal capital movements. In the *Balance of Payments Manual* this concept was introduced with enthusiasm, but there is a danger that it may be applied with a considerable lack of discrimination. Any attempt to squeeze the transactions of countries at different times and in different economic circumstances into rigidly defined categories may lead to a superficial but misleading simplification. On the other hand British classificatory practice is perhaps less consistent than is desirable and appears on occasion to be guided too much by current and passing considerations. This is perhaps a natural result of the way in which the White Paper is produced as a by-product of policy-making.

CONCLUSION

We have not tried to discuss in this chapter the whole of the relation of statistics to foreign trade and payments policy. There are, for instance, the questions of policy connected with the exchange rate, or with extensions of convertibility, which might each require special statistical work to bring out their implications. But the problems of the balance of payments have been so difficult for so long that it is likely that the Treasury and the Bank make excellent use of the information available to them. Some of this information is born of their own administration, notably exchange control, and might cease to exist because of future administrative changes; we should like to see more clearly what action

[1] R. G. D. Allen [86].

is then to be taken to maintain the flow of information. We are inclined to think that the necessary secrecy about acts of administration is allowed too easily to become also a secrecy about methods. The country has reason to be grateful to the ingenuity of the official statisticians who have created estimates of the balance-of-payments position which are probably as good as any in the world. But it has no sufficient means of judging the quality of work whose methods are never explained to those outside. We cannot think that this is a healthy state of affairs.

CHAPTER IX

THE GENERAL BALANCE OF THE ECONOMY

In examining particular instances of the uses of economic statistics in relation to policy, we turn last to what is sometimes called 'overall' or general planning. State intervention in economic affairs has a long history, which shows changes from time to time in both the objectives and the methods of the intervention. What is new in the practice of State intervention in the last few years is the conscious attempt to make a co-ordinated and 'scientific' use of the Government's means of affecting the economy. An overall picture of economic processes is given in the social accounts; this sort of accountancy has grown up to serve the needs of a State which believes in its duty to exercise a planned control over the economy, and the great extension of knowledge embodied in those accounts has given the 'planner' a confidence, probably excessive, in his ability to plan.

As we have seen, the use of the term 'planning' in this connexion does not imply detailed regulation of individual economic enterprises, such as is popularly supposed to occur in a Socialist or 'mixed' economy. The work of the Council of Economic Advisers in the United States and the ideas embodied in the President's Economic Reports to Congress are included, just as much as the 'Economic Surveys' in Britain. Britain, however, illustrates in an acute form the problems involved in general economic direction. The 1944 White Paper on *Employment Policy*[1] stated that 'the Government accept as one of their primary aims and responsibilities the maintenance of a high and stable level of employment after the war'. That White Paper was, however, mainly concerned with the maintenance of total expenditure and with the means by which the components of expenditure might be stimulated. It gave full recognition to the possible need for restraining expenditure in a boom; but (like much economic thought at that time) it was much influenced by the fear that, after the war, Britain might again have the high rate of unemployment of the inter-war period.

The experience of the succeeding years has reminded us that the British economy cannot be 'managed' by aiming at some simple objective, such as the maintenance of full employment. There are instead a large number of conflicting objects of policy, and the right way of deciding the relative 'weights' to be assigned to them is so far very much a matter of personal judgement. The main objects are:

[1] [58].

(i) The maintenance of a satisfactory balance of payments position.

(ii) The maintenance of full employment.

(iii) The prevention of rapid rises in internal prices.

(iv) The maintenance and steady increase of productivity.

(v) Adequate expansion of capital.

(vi) The maintenance of consumption standards, especially those of the poor.

These can be summed up by saying that the Government has to perform a double balancing feat—externally, keeping a healthy balance of payments, and internally, treading the narrow way between the ditch of Depression and the dangerous quag of Inflation. It has to do this by means which preserve an orderly progress—neither lessening too much the incentive to work in the present, nor creating excessive inequalities of income, nor laying too heavy restrictions on the growth of capital, on which the wealth of the future depends. But what is 'too much', 'excessive' or 'too heavy' is a matter on which judgements will of course differ.

THE ECONOMIC SURVEY

The difficult and complex process described above is, of course, being undertaken throughout the year. But the Budget has come to be regarded as one of the principal regulators of the economy, and a special interest therefore attaches to the calculations which are used by the Chancellor in deciding his Budget policy. In the post-war years a good deal of the background of these decisions was publicly revealed in the annual *Economic Surveys*, which were, except in 1952, debated by Parliament at the time of the Budget.

The pattern of the *Economic Surveys* has been to review the past year, and to forecast the principal economic variables for the current one.[1] The 'forecast' is in part a mere extrapolation from past experience; thus, since the *Survey* is normally published before the Budget, it assumes unchanged tax rates in any estimation of Government revenue. In part, however, the *Survey's* forecasts are revelations of policy, or of what the Government considers necessary and intends to bring about. As the visible part of an iceberg is but a little of the whole mass, so the information cautiously revealed in the *Survey* rests on a much larger structure of departmental and Cabinet policy-making. In this structure statistical information is an essential part; and we have therefore studied, as fully as we could, the processes which lie behind the *Survey* and the Budget policy.

As we have already observed, it is not possible to describe the precise way in which the decisions entering into a document such as the

---

[1] The forecasts, originally quantitative, have been reduced in the 1952 and 1953 *Surveys* to vague indications of direction of motion. But this is partly a matter of presentation; we shall discuss the quantitative forecasting which presumably still goes on behind the scenes.

Economic Survey are made. The process of decision-making is in any case confidential, and things have to be considered other than those expressed in economic statistics. The details must vary greatly from year to year, according to the personalities of those engaged and the political judgements made. But behind it all lies a 'model', a set of equations, from which the appropriate magnitudes of Government action can be deduced. Since the 'input' into the model consists of estimates with substantial margins of error, the 'output' will also not be definite, but will have a range of indeterminacy. The use of the non-economic factors is sometimes to fix a definite place on this range provided by the economic model; but since (when definite figures were given) it was the custom to publish, not ranges within which figures were expected to lie, but single figures, this process was concealed from view.

THE 'MODEL' FOR THE ECONOMIC SURVEY

The model can in practice be put together in many different ways, and is set up in different ways in different years, according to the nature of the 'planning' being practised and the relative accuracy of the statistical estimates which can be fed into it. One way has been described by Mr E. F. Jackson,[1] and in a simple form it may be expressed in a diagram as follows:

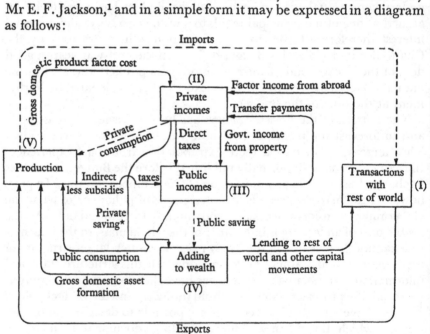

— — — — – Residual estimates   * Including depreciation provisions

[1] Jackson [100]; the diagram is due to Mr Richard Stone.

The arrows in the diagram are money flows, and they are seen passing through five points at which inflows and outflows must balance. Thus (I) is the balance of payments:

Imports plus net lending = Exports plus net factor income from overseas.

The system is a closed one, so that if balance is achieved at four of the points it must be achieved at the fifth. Having decided to build a model out of these simple constituents, the choices to be made are as follows:

(a) In which order shall we take the equations of the system, so as to determine successively the items which are 'unknown' or which have to be fixed by Government action?

(b) At each stage, which flows shall we take as 'known' and which as 'residuals in the model'[1] to be determined from the equation?

The order described by Mr Jackson is as follows; the illustrative figures are invented, in order to avoid the complications of describing an actual *Economic Survey* with its various price assumptions.

			£(mn.)
Stage 1:	Forecasts of Exports		3,300
		Factor incomes from abroad (net)	200
	less	Intended net rate of foreign lending	−300
	Hence: Permissible rate of imports		£3,200
Stage 2:	Forecasts of Gross domestic product, factor cost		12,000
		Transfer incomes	1,350
		Factor incomes from abroad	200
	less	Government income from property	−200
		Direct taxes	−1,900
		Private saving and depreciation provisions	−2,150
	Hence: Expected level of private consumption		£9,300
Stage 3(a):	Forecasts of Indirect taxes (mainly a function of private consumption)		1,300
		Direct taxes	1,900
		Government income from property	200
	less	Government current expenditure	−2,000
		Transfer payments	−1,350
	Hence: Expected public saving		£50
Stage 3(b):	'Planned' rate of Gross asset formation at home		2,500
		Foreign lending	300
	less	Private saving and depreciation provisions	−2,150
	Hence: Required public saving		£650

At the second part of Stage 3, the funds available to finance capital formation are compared with the use to be made of them. Except by a rare accident, the implied rate of public saving will not equal the expected rate from Stage 3 (a); it will not even be within the margin

_____
[1] See pp. 99–100 below.

allowed by the uncertainty of the component estimates. A choice has to be made—either to operate on one of the items of Stage 3 (*b*) directly (for example by changing the planned rate of asset formation at home or overseas), or to go further back and alter items in the other equations. Such alterations will normally have secondary effects, and the whole system will have to be re-worked until it reaches an approximate state of balance.

Thus, in the example shown, indirect taxes might be increased by £200 million, producing a fall in private saving of £100 million, and gross asset formation at home might be cut to £2000 million.

Stage 1, the foreign balance, we suppose unchanged; the others become:

		£ (mn.)
Stage 2:	Domestic product	12,000
	Transfers	1,350
	Factor incomes from abroad	200
	Government property income	−200
	Direct taxes	−1,900
	Private saving	−2,050
	Private consumption	£9,400

Stage 3(*a*):		£ (mn.)	Stage 3(*b*):		£ (mn.)
	Indirect taxes	1,500		Gross asset forma-	2,000
	Direct taxes	1,900		tion at home	
	Government property income	200		Foreign lending	300
				Private saving	−2,050
	Government current expenditure	−2,000			
	Transfer payments	−1,350			
	Public saving	£250		Public saving	£250

There is, of course, automatic agreement at the remaining point of balance:

	£ (mn.)		£ (mn.)
Gross domestic product (factor cost)	12,000	Private consumption	9,400
Imports	3,200	Government current expenditure	2,000
Indirect taxes	1,500	Gross asset formation	2,000
		Exports	3,300
	£16,700		£16,700

Four comments may be made on this process:

(i) A consistent system, when it is attained, may not be a possible one. It may, for instance, have built into it a rate of private consumption which could be held only by restrictions on the consumer which are politically impossible. The solution to this (which has been adopted in some years) is to estimate private consumption and treat saving as a residual. Or, again, the implied rate of imports might be insufficient to sustain the rate of production—more realistically, the necessary raw material imports might be able to be financed only by an impossibly severe restriction of food imports. The 'residuals', therefore, are not free to vary as they will; acceptable answers have to lie within a certain range.

(ii) The choice of 'residuals' can be made in different ways. There are items which, in a freely operating system, would naturally take the first shock of adjustment; thus, in the balance of payments, it would normally be the capital movements which (by the running up or down of foreign balances) would be the primary adjusters. There is reason to regard at least part of private saving as being residual, appearing after consumption has been satisfied. But the system shown above chooses instead items capable of being influenced more directly by changes of Government policy—imports, private consumption, public saving. This supposes that one knows a 'normal' level of variables which are 'naturally' residuals—a hazardous process of estimation.

(iii) The flows used are money flows, and they involve price assumptions. In fact, as Jackson points out,[1] inconsistent price assumptions are sometimes made in the *Survey*. There may in any case be a choice to be made between assuming a price level which is thought to be desirable (but unlikely to be achieved), and assuming a price level which is (on the little evidence available) thought likely, but not desirable. If import prices have risen in the preceding year, is one to assume that in the coming year wages will rise in sympathy, and produce further price rises?

(iv) The estimates included are uncertain—some of them very uncertain. Their 'errors' are related to one another, because they form a balancing system. Nevertheless the size of the adjustment finally required must also be uncertain. This uncertainty may be obscured by the bad habit[2] of showing single estimates with no indication of margins of error. We shall give further attention to this point in the next section.

THE STATISTICAL REQUIREMENTS—GENERAL

A discussion of the statistical requirements for a model such as this is liable to be confused because of difficulties of terminology. We shall keep to the following definitions for the rest of this chapter:

(a) Figures which describe what actually happened in *past* periods of time will be called *estimates*. The aura of uncertainty surrounding this word is appropriate, for none of the figures will be completely certain. One can distinguish various degrees of uncertainty—good estimates, such as Government expenditure in 1951, and doubtful estimates,

---

[1] [100], p. 157.   [2] Jackson agrees ([100], p. 151).

such as capital formation in the form of alterations or improvements to premises. One can also distinguish *residual estimates*, that is, figures which for past years are found only as residuals required to make the equations 'add up'. For instance, there is a residual capital transfer item in the balance of payments. These residuals are chosen as the items most difficult to estimate directly; they will thus differ in different years (according to the judgements of the statisticians about the weakest links in their system), and they will also usually differ from the 'residuals in the model' which, as we have seen above, are chosen in a different way.

(*b*) Figures relating to the *present and future*—for example to the calendar year current at the time of publication of a *Survey*—need careful analysis. We can distinguish:

(i) *Forecasts* obtained (for instance) by projecting past trends, by correlation, or by bringing together an assortment of known commitments, guesses, hunches, assumptions and trend projections. For instance, there will be a *forecast* of gross domestic product at constant prices, compounded of various assumptions and ideas about the size of the labour force and its productivity, amended in the light of knowledge about 'real factors' expected to affect particular industries. A forecast may be 'realistic'—that is to say, it may represent the honest opinion of the compiler about what is likely to happen; or it may have built into it assumptions, for example constancy of prices, which may be the object of policy but are not likely to be realized in full.

(ii) *Assumptions*, often embodying the expected results of acts of policy already announced. Just as a forecast often contains an element of assumption, so an assumption is bounded by forecasts of what could conceivably happen; it would be no use, for instance, assuming that exports would suddenly double their volume. A quantity such as the change in sterling balances fluctuates so wildly that one could hardly predict its behaviour from what has happened in the past: it is assumed that, in the working out of policies currently being applied, the change will reach a certain figure.

(iii) *Dummy figures*. These arise when the model has to be prepared or published in advance of some major policy decision. Thus when the *Survey* is published before the Budget it shows the yields of taxation on the basis of the tax rates of the financial year then just ending. The model then contains inconsistencies or improbabilities which may be expected to be removed when the Budget has been opened and the dummy figures can be replaced by forecasts or assumptions.

(iv) *Residuals in the model*. These need no further explanation.

The possible divergence suggested at the end of (i), between what one hopes and what one expects, is worth a moment's consideration. Policy should, of course, be founded on realistic expectations. But, especially in its earlier years, the *Economic Survey* was conceived as a means of publicity as well as of analysis. To say 'we expect textile exports to be worth £350 million' would be a hindrance if one was urging the industry to export to a value of £450 million; effort might be relaxed when the 'expected' figure was reached. A *published* description of a model may, therefore, contain what are known as 'target figures' which are expressions of hope rather than of expectation. The inclusion of such figures should, of course, produce inconsistencies elsewhere—for example, if exports are put too high the required inflow of capital may be put too low—but these will not be easy to trace.

One more general point about the statistical foundation of the *Survey* model is worth remembering. The model is designed to help in making *changes* of policy—for example changes in the tax burden. Although the totals of exports, imports, the national product, etc., all appear, what is really important is the year-to-year changes. Thus, if the gross product were in all years estimated and forecast £300 million too small, with a corresponding error in the estimate or residual forecast of private consumption, the effect on policy-making would be negligible. But it would be important if the error were negative when the gross product was rising and positive when it was falling; for then the estimate of change at a turning-point would be very much in error, and the effect on policy might be disastrous.

From one point of view this emphasis on changes rather than on absolute quantities is a relief: there is reason to suspect that some of the errors in national income aggregates may be of the type of a nearly constant omission or bias in all years. But the change in a quantity which is itself found as the difference between two larger quantities may be liable to wide errors; thus, in the years in which private consumption has been forecast and saving found as a residual, the resulting figure of saving is a most uncertain one. Furthermore, it is natural to think of the forecast *change* as being the last link in a chain, whose previous links are the differences between estimates for earlier years. But if these estimates have been made independently from year to year, perhaps even by different methods, the earlier links in the chain may be subject to much error, and be a very poor basis for extrapolation. The whole process of basing changes of policy on changes of £100 million or so in aggregates of £10,000 million or more is suspect; it forcibly illustrates the need for more knowledge and understanding of the margins of error of the estimates and forecasts—in particular, of the way in which the errors of different items are related. This is a point to which we shall return in Chapter x.

We will now examine briefly the different statistical estimates required for the model in its simple form described above. In practice, of course, some breakdown into economic sectors is made, so as to ensure (for instance) that the assumed use of metal goods does not outrun the supplies of iron and steel. In the future it may be possible, by the techniques of input-output analysis and activity analysis, to treat the problem of equilibrium in a much more detailed way; at present only rudimentary attention is given to limiting 'real' factors and to problems of balance between different industries or sectors. The *Economic Survey* has thus become mainly an exercise in the use of the broad economic aggregates which appear in the national income estimates. A proper official description of the methods used in obtaining British national income statistics, and a discussion of their margins of error, has been much needed.[1] The methods change with bewildering rapidity, and it is extremely difficult for laymen to follow the changes; they are perhaps inevitable in the early years of development of new methods, but they make it difficult to study the nature and quality of the figures properly. We hope that a period of stability is now in sight, and that staff will be available to give full descriptions of the methods used.

THE BALANCE OF PAYMENTS

Since this is the subject of Chapter VIII, it needs only a summary treatment here. The basis of information for past periods is, on the face of it, good; the British statistics of visible trade are of good quality, and appear with commendable speed; the half-yearly Balance of Payments White Paper has become steadily clearer and more informative. Nevertheless the forecasting of the items of the balance of payments is, as experience shows, a hazardous affair. 'Foreign' variables, such as the level of U.S. national income, enter in as well as domestic ones; changes in the price or output of our competitors in foreign markets will affect our trade; and our knowledge of income and price elasticities in foreign trade is still small. But the worst difficulty arises in forecasting the invisible and capital items, especially those which are mainly affected by Britain's position as banker to the sterling area. Some are the direct object of policy decisions, and can be 'assumed'—for example the rate of use of sterling balances by certain countries—but since the decisions are partly a matter for Governments outside the United Kingdom the reliability of the assumptions will be difficult to assess. The private investigator is unable to do much serious forecasting in the rest of this field; the White Papers 'lump together' so many items (to avoid disclosure) that they give little help. But the Government must, of course, have available to it a much greater mass of information, mainly collected by the Bank

---

[1] The gap will, we understand, be partly filled by an O.E.E.C. publication in 1953.

of England and passed by the Bank to the Treasury. The Bank's statistical operations are surrounded by barriers of secrecy which we have not been able to penetrate, and we can therefore say nothing about the quality of the material which is produced. As far as published information goes, we have mentioned above our regret that the balance unaccounted for peeps shyly from its seclusion in the item 'Other capital transactions (net)',[1] so that we cannot even judge the quality of the statistics by looking at the internal consistency of the balance-of-payments accounts.

We have no evidence which would justify us in any criticism of the statistics which we suppose to be available to the Treasury in forecasting the balance of payments. But we repeat our view that the whole matter is surrounded by unnecessary secrecy, and that it is not wise for the country to rely, in this important matter, on a small group of people who are entirely protected from the criticism of other qualified professional statisticians.

THE GROSS PRODUCT

A starting point for forecasting the national product is provided by the estimates for previous years given in the National Income White Papers. These estimates are probably subject to a good deal of error—and there are certainly large revisions of the figures from time to time—but we have no means of assessing how far the errors may affect the year-to-year changes.

In a particular year—say in the spring of 1953—the estimates of national product for 1952 are based on incomplete data, so that it would not be sufficient to make a forecast by a simple extrapolation of the trends of past years. Such an extrapolation would in any case mix up the price and the real output changes. What we want initially is a forecast of national product in 1953 at some fixed price level—such as that of the end of 1952. There is a partial indicator of changes in output in the monthly index of industrial production. A certain amount is known about the likely relation between industrial and total domestic product,[2] but there are few up-to-date indicators in the non-industrial field. It becomes necessary, then, to bring together a number of scraps of information, and to make guesses about the extent to which known or expected 'special' influences—for example a raw material shortage— may change the trend of production. The forecast cannot be strengthened to any great extent by considering figures of the money national product deflated by a price index; for there are difficult statistical problems involved in that deflation which are only just beginning to receive

[1] P. 84 above.   [2] See Reddaway [112] and Carter [91].

systematic treatment. In principle, the forecasting of real product could be done in a more scientific and detailed way if there were available for the United Kingdom more 'input-output' studies;[1] but this form of research is still in its infancy here, and many of its problems, both theoretical and practical, have still to be solved.

A forecast at fixed prices having been obtained, a forecast embodying any other desired price assumption can be prepared. But it can be seen that the forecast of the extra product to be expected from the economy as a whole is a doubtful one; the origin of that extra product, by industries, is also difficult to foresee, and it is almost impossible to assess the way in which the associated extra income will be divided between the factors of production. The division ought to be known if careful forecasts of consumption and saving are to be made, but it depends on the ebb and flow of the struggles between the different factors, and the timing and extent of the movements are wholly uncertain. But before we conclude prematurely that the whole process which employs these uncertain forecasts and guesses is useless, we must reflect that to leave the Government's actions to be settled without any of the statistical background would be worse still. The imperfections look serious when compared with an ideal state of perfect knowledge; but fitful gleams of moonlight are a great deal better to walk by than complete darkness.

PRIVATE CONSUMPTION

In some years this is a 'residual in the model', in others it is forecast directly and private saving is taken as a residual; but a direct forecast will in any case be needed to fix the bounds within which a 'tolerable' residual may lie. Or we may, instead of estimating consumption and personal saving from their own past trends, estimate personal disposable income and the *proportions* taken by consumption and saving.

'Private' consumption, which is mostly 'personal' or 'household' consumption, depends on many factors—the size of the population and of its age-distribution, the distribution of incomes, the recent history of prices and expectations of future prices, memories of past consumption, and so on. There are serious difficulties, both of principle and of practice, in forecasting its year-to-year changes. Statistics exist for the past, in the C.S.O. quarterly estimates of consumer expenditure and their revaluation at fixed prices; and there are scraps of information in the retail trade statistics and other figures for goods in late stages of distribution. These various statistics of the past are imperfect, and their errors may not be random. But if we use them as a basis for a forecast of

[1] See Barna T. [88] and *National Income and Expenditure, 1946–1951* [34c], p. 24.

consumption, and assume stable prices and no tax changes, we still have three problems to solve:

(a) What autonomous changes are taking place within the pattern of consumption? Some forms of expenditure will be contracting and some expanding.

(b) How will income be distributed between factors of production and between different social or income groups? Admittedly, a knowledge of this would at present not lead us very far, for we know all too little about the pattern of expenditure of different groups.

(c) Will the past history of saving tend to cause exceptional saving or dissaving in the current year? After a year of heavy and unexpected dissaving, for instance, consumption might be restricted as people struggle to build up savings stocks.

The answers to these questions will be doubtful, and it is probably not possible to obtain more than a rough forecast. But that forecast will itself be unstable; for if the assumption of stable prices breaks down, all the elements of income distribution, the pattern of expenditure, and the habits of saving will alter. There may be a 'buyers' strike', or a 'buyers' spree'; the 'textile slump' of 1951–2 illustrates how difficult it may be, in those circumstances, to estimate either the extent or the duration of the change in consumer demand. In practice, therefore, a forecast by extrapolation of past trends in consumption may be so rough that it will be necessary to have recourse to an assumption—such as constancy of consumption. We are not in sight of the time when it will be possible to build up a forecast of consumption by applying the results of demand analysis to an expected or assumed pattern of income or prices.

GROSS PRIVATE SAVING

There are several elements in this; they are shown in (for example) Tables 8 and 9 of the 1952 National Income Blue Book (34c):

	1951 £(mn.)
Provision for depreciation	756
Other sums set aside by companies and public corporations	1,221
less Provision for stock appreciation	−1,100
Gross personal saving (incl. additions to tax reserves)	178
	£1,055

Provision for depreciation by public authorities can be taken as part of 'public saving'; and it will be convenient to consider the problem of estimating stock appreciation as though it were an addition to capital formation rather than a subtraction from saving. Furthermore, since capital formation is to be estimated gross, there is no need to concern ourselves with the (admittedly arbitrary) depreciation provisions. We can consider

	1951 £(mn.)
Gross private non-personal saving (=depreciation provisions plus other sums set aside)	1,977
Gross personal saving	178
	£2,155

Additions to tax reserves can be added, or can be regarded as part of 'public saving'—the heading in Table 29 is 'Sums set aside through the action of public authorities'.

There is no reason to expect that personal saving will be a stable function of total personal income after tax. It consists of two main parts: contractual saving (life insurance premiums, pension contributions, etc.) and non-contractual saving. The non-contractual part, which may at times be negative, is for some individuals 'planned' at a certain figure—it may be accidental that it takes a non-contractual form; but for many people non-contractual saving emerges as an unplanned residue or deficit when other needs have been met. It depends, not only on the total of income and its distribution, but on the past history and future prospects of prices.

The information about personal saving is extremely scrappy and disjointed; it is almost confined to the so-called 'small savings' (now often negative) in National Savings Certificates, Defence Bonds and Savings Banks, and to insurance premiums and payments to Building Societies. The only way out is to make some broad assumption, such as constancy in money terms.

At present, however, non-personal saving is much the larger part of private saving; and it depends largely on the level of profits. Leaving on one side the problem of finding the profits of private companies and partnerships, except after a time-lag of at least two years, it is clearly very difficult to forecast the profits of public companies. For published profit figures will appear, on an average, some ten months after the middle of the period to which they relate; so that a White Paper to be completed in March 1953 will not have full published profit figures relating to 1952, and must rely on the result of special inquiries. *Forecasts* of company profit will be highly sensitive to the assumptions made about prices, and may go badly astray.

The savings we require are

(Profits before depreciation allowances + Other income
    – Tax payments – Payments of dividends and interest).

'Other income' includes receipts of public debt interest by companies, and actual or imputed income from the ownership of land and buildings; items of this sort are likely to be relatively stable. Tax payments can be forecast; and any error in them will produce an equal and opposite error in public saving, so accuracy is not so important. Dividend and interest payments follow quite a smooth trend, and they are known a little *before* the actual payments are made; there should be little difficulty in forecasting them, except perhaps at a turning-point.

The problem of finding private savings therefore reduces, for the most part, to a problem of forecasting profits. For if we abandon company accounts and try to forecast the change in non-personal savings from more general considerations, we are back to the problem of allocating the change in total incomes between the factors of production. The whole problem is so difficult that it may well be better to choose the alternative path, and treat savings as a 'residual in the model' instead of private consumption.

THE GOVERNMENT ITEMS

Direct and indirect tax receipts, transfer payments, and public consumption all come into the model. There should be no great difficulty of principle, at the official level, in forecasting these, and the 'estimates' for a year or so back will be firm accounting figures. The main problem will arise in dealing with local authority current expenditure, for which no official 'estimates' for the future are collected; and there is a very long delay in bringing together final local authority accounts. This, however, is a stable item, and data may be available from the Associations of local authorities. It may also be difficult to use the Central Government Estimates, on a cash basis, for a financial year, to derive expenditure properly attributable to a calendar, or some other, year. The private investigator in this field is likely to be baffled by the extraordinary unevenness of treatment in the Central Government Estimates, which account in meticulous detail for tiny sums while lumping tens of millions of pounds under some vague and general heading. No doubt, however, the Government does not allow itself to be misled by the imperfections of its own presentation of accounts.

GROSS DOMESTIC CAPITAL FORMATION

The call on resources for domestic capital formation can of course be estimated and forecast 'gross'; it is unaffected by the arbitrary allowance for depreciation. The figures for fixed capital formation in the National Income Blue Book are built up from detailed estimates for certain major industries, and a figure for capital formation in manufacturing industry which was for some time obtained from a special sample survey of investment, but is now derived from advance Census of Production data. The detailed estimates are partly obtained from the 'output' side—for example for building and civil engineering and for vehicles, and partly from returns made by nationalized or 'controlled' industries—coal, steel, gas, electricity, the Transport Commission, etc. (It will be noted that information will be lacking for 'service trades' not capable of being surveyed directly and outside the scope of the Census of Production.) One might think that some of the monthly production series for machinery and vehicles would provide up-to-date indicators; but, with a few exceptions (e.g. commercial vehicles), it is difficult to identify the final use as being domestic capital formation within the period concerned.

The statistics of fixed capital formation are, however, probably quite good for years since 1948. In forecasting the total for a current year one can make use of some information from the demand and supply sides about investment intentions—for example for nationalized industry— and about order books in engineering and shipbuilding. But there is no general collection of data on investment intentions from private industry, such as exists in the United States. This is a serious gap. It is true that some experience would be required before one could know the bias which is likely to exist in people's statements of investment intentions; but the statistics would at least give warning of marked changes of trend —information which at present has to be obtained from City gossip and general knowledge of business conditions, supplemented by scraps of information about, for example, applications for building licences.

The statistics of investment in stocks and work in progress are much less satisfactory. There is little systematic knowledge of the changes in work in progress likely to be associated with a given change in the pattern of production—for example the building-up of the rearmament programme. With the exception of Government-held stocks, for which both past history and future intentions are presumably known, the information about stocks is extremely slight. Such figures as exist (for example for a section of retail trade) are commonly in value terms, the basis of valuation being uncertain. These gaps are serious, and the filling of them should have a high priority; but they are more important when one wants, *ex post*, to discover how the national product has been used. The remarkable figure for stock appreciation in 1951 shown in (**34c**)—£1,100 million[1]—with its accompanying implication that there must have been large corporate dissaving in that year, must be regarded as resting on flimsy statistical evidence. The gap is especially unfortunate, because small percentage changes in stocks may be large by value in relation to changes in fixed capital formation.

[1] Revised to £900 million in Cmd. 8803 [**34d**].

SUMMING UP

Our sketchy examination of the co-ordinated and scientific use of statistical information to serve the State's responsibility to secure balance in the economy has not been an encouraging one. The result looks about as scientific as Alice's celebrated attempt to play croquet by hitting a live hedgehog with a flamingo. It looks doubtful if such a procedure could be successful in the important task of forecasting *turning-points* of the economy so that policy can be adapted in good time. On the statistical side, we have noticed important gaps in the information available, for example on stocks or investment intentions; we have seen cause to suspect that errors may be large, for example in forecasting visible trade. In addition to the errors of forecasting, there will be imperfections in the past estimates which are used in deriving the forecasts. Some of them are too far in the past; others are little more than guesses, for example some of the 'service' items of consumer expenditure.

In addition to these statistical defects, there are serious econometric difficulties. We know very little about many of the important parameters which express the interrelations in our model of the system. This is not a readily removable difficulty. If we simplify the model further it will lose touch with reality—it is already treating as simple variables complex aggregates such as 'consumption' whose parts may move very differently. Yet there is seldom a satisfactory period, of stable institutional structure and stable external circumstances, which one can use to obtain good estimates of parameters. In practice, one constantly appeals to the experience of the past year or two, ignoring perforce many circumstances of those years which were exceptional.

Yet there is no doubt that, both on the statistical and on the econometric side, great improvement is possible through further investigation and research. The post-war attempts at 'overall planning' in Britain may not have been notably successful; but it is arguable that the alternative of sailing blind into the seas of economic circumstance is probably[1] much worse. The imperfections which we have discussed serve to remind us of a need which so far we have not mentioned in this chapter—the need for determining policy, not only by occasional assessments of the general position, but by constant attention to indicators of disequilibrium and of economic progress. We must turn now to see if those available are adequate.

[1] Not certainly; bad statistics may be worse than none at all, if people believe them.

INDICATORS OF DISEQUILIBRIUM AND PROGRESS

The obvious primary indicators of domestic disequilibrium are the statistics of unemployment and of prices.[1] Both are reasonably good, and price statistics are steadily being improved; but, as one might expect, they do not always give definite and timely warning of disequilibrium. It is difficult to distinguish 'general' unemployment from the 'transitional' unemployment associated with a change in the pattern of production—indeed, the logical distinction between the two is not clear, and consequently it is impossible to say whether a rise in unemployment to (say) 350,000 is a signal to reverse deflationary measures or merely a necessary accompaniment of flexibility. It would be useful to have more detailed information about labour turnover; the gross rates of turnover are difficult to interpret, and it should be possible (by a sample investigation) to learn much more about mobility between firms, industries and places, and to find out whether it is true that much unemployment causes, or is associated with, a movement from one industry to another.

Employment and unemployment statistics may therefore be late in giving definite indication of a slump; and it is natural to ask whether 'advance warnings' can be found of a change in the state of demand. The determination of turning-points is a subject much studied by business cycle experts in the United States. But in Britain systematic work is hampered by the relatively unsatisfactory state of the retail and wholesale trade statistics, by the lack of many reliable figures for stocks and stock changes, and by the absence of information about the state of order books. Some improvement should be possible when the results of the first Census of Distribution have been fully used, but some will have to wait until more econometric research—particularly demand analysis —has been done. Thus, it was possible to forecast the 'textile slump' of 1951–2 from an examination of retail and wholesale trade statistics in the preceding months, but not (on present information) to say how serious it would be. On the Stock Exchange, changes in the primary trend of prices are often preceded by a change in the ratio of gilt-edged to ordinary share yields, but such aids to forecasting are rare in other markets.

The appearance of serious inflationary tendencies can be seen in the price statistics—and the improvement of wholesale price statistics will help observation at an early stage. But it takes some time for inflation to 'work its way through' into retail prices, and, by the time it has done so, it is already stimulating further rises in factor prices. A direct watch on factor prices can be kept in the case of wages and earnings; but profits can only be followed after a time-lag (averaging 9–10 months

---

[1] And stocks; but the statistics, as we have seen, are rudimentary.

between the date of earning and the date of declaration), and information on salaries is scanty. Some evidence can be obtained from financial statistics, which are abundant and on the whole good; however, short-term variations in (say) bank deposits or bank advances are frequently difficult to interpret.

In general we can say that indicators of internal disequilibrium exist in fair volume—though improvements could be made, and some are suggested above. But the implications for policy will often be somewhat uncertain. What do we make of 1952, for instance, when production was falling but unemployment remained generally low? Furthermore, the impact of changes in external prices on the British economy is considerable, and it is difficult to sort out 'import-induced' price rises from those of domestic origin.

The chief indicator of the external position has come to be the size of the gold and dollar reserve. This is (as it were) a thermometer, which indicates whether the patient is in danger, but does not of itself tell us how to diagnose or cure his disease. Good short-term statistics of visible trade exist, and are quickly available, and the Bank of England no doubt has some short-term information about movements in invisibles and capital items. It must, however, be difficult to keep an eye on the use of gold and dollars made by other members of the sterling area. Their trade statistics are in some cases slow to appear, and it seems that when large changes take place it is some months before the situation can be assessed and appropriate action taken.

The short-term and partial indicators would be more useful if we could have a more frequent general check on the situation by repeating each quarter the analysis which we have outlined in the 'model' above. Quarterly estimates of consumption are available, and a quarterly Revenue Account of Public Authorities could no doubt be produced; the balance of payments is calculated by half-years, and might perhaps be estimated by quarters; and it should be possible to obtain quarterly estimates of national product (subject to some difficult conceptual problems, for example in farming). Quarterly estimates of investment would be a new departure, but we should like to see them attempted.

In all this we must not forget that equilibrium must not be bought at the price of stagnation: there is need for indicators of progress as well. Production statistics could be improved, both by extensions into the non-industrial field and by fuller use of the information on input. (At present, calculations of 'value added at constant prices' often have to assume that this is proportional to the gross quantity, or deflated value, of output; thus assuming input a constant proportion of output.) There is a need for more studies of productivity—using this term in a general sense, to include production per unit of any scarce factor. The work of the Girdwood Committee[1] on the extent and causes of changes in apparent labour productivity in house-building is a good example of the type of research required.

CONCLUSION

This chapter, in outlining the statistics available to, or needed by, those in charge of general economic policy, has revealed a good many weaknesses and difficulties. These exist in almost any statistical system; they involve no modification of our judgement that British statistics are among the best in the world; it suggests rather that one should be cautious in one's claim of what statistical knowledge can achieve. Caution is, indeed, visible in the increasing vagueness of the *Economic Surveys*; but this is partly perhaps due to a fear of publishing forecasts which are not likely to be accurate, rather than to an unwillingness to use them behind the scenes. Indeed, policy has to call on the available numerical information, if not to determine its precise form, at least to suggest rough orders of magnitude. It seems to us very important that the estimates and forecasts we have been discussing should be improved before they are strained by more violent changes of economic circumstance.

[1] [61].

CHAPTER X

THE QUALITY OF ECONOMIC STATISTICS

It is rare indeed to find a piece of statistical information that is 'perfect', in the double sense of being observed without error and of being precisely suited to its purpose. Even the elaborate and expensive organization of a census of population can never tell you exactly how many people were in the country on the census night; still less can it tell you what you usually want to know, the populations 'normally resident' in each area. Those who prepare the raw material of statistical investigation are often modest in their claims about the accuracy of their figures; they know only too well how, despite careful planning, errors creep in and gaps have to be filled by guesswork. Those whose duty it is to use this raw material to analyse situations or to prepare plans of action must usually be conscious of the failure of their materials to conform to the precise specifications they require. For instance, imports are recorded c.i.f. but for some purposes must be 'reduced' to f.o.b.: and this reduction involves estimates of freight rates with a substantial margin of error.

As previous chapters have shown, it seemed to us at many points in our investigation that the treatment of error in British economic statistics is inadequate. People who may be scrupulously honest in acknowledging the imperfections of figures which they prepare themselves seem disposed to turn a charitable blind eye to the imperfections of figures handed up to them. An 'estimate' which started in one office as little more than a guess is liable (by the time it has passed through three or four hands) to be quoted as though it were an observed fact. The qualifications which the honest originator had in mind, and perhaps stated in small type at the foot of his tables, have been forgotten. 'This', the final user seems to say, 'is the only estimate I can find. Better the moonlight than complete darkness: let us hope that the errors will cancel out.'

This tendency is assisted by the supposed preference of Practical Men for single estimates. Suppose, for instance, that a Chancellor of the Exchequer, in performing (as we have described on p. 97 above) his annual exercise of using the Budget to secure balance in the economy, were to substitute for all the single estimates of national income, investment, Government expenditure and so on the margins within which the true figures are believed (by their originators) to lie. He would no longer be able to lay before the House of Commons reasoned arguments for (say) increasing taxation by £300 million; for his estimate of the proper increase of taxation would now itself have a range, perhaps from minus £100 million to plus £600 million, and this range could only be narrowed by a careful examination of the likely relation between the errors in the constituent items of the final estimate.

To those who have to make a definite policy decision, and to justify it to a critical public without expert knowledge of the facts, such vagueness would seem intolerable. Yet it is not enough to hope that a figure derived from a number of 'best estimates' made by different people will by itself be a sound foundation for decision. An understanding of the errors to which the various constituent figures are subject might show that they are not random in their effects on the final estimate, but are correlated, perhaps making the final estimate unstable and subject to much error. Even if one could say, with fair assurance, that deviations on each side of the final figure were equally *likely*, it would not follow that they would be equally dangerous. Thus in a particular situation the dangers of inflation might be greater than those associated with deflation; there might be reason to suppose that an inflationary impulse, given to the economy, would multiply itself and have disastrous effects on the foreign balance, while a deflationary impulse would be heavily damped (perhaps by the spending of part of some large public holdings of encashable assets). In such a situation a Chancellor ought not to be encouraged to have regard to a single 'best estimate' of his proper Budget surplus; he ought to know something about the chances of his estimate proving too low.

We do not suppose that so elementary and important a point will have gone unnoticed by the Treasury and the Cabinet Office. But we do think that there is evidence that there is too little examination of the quality of statistics. The present situation has been defended to us mainly on the grounds that, without laborious research involving time and money which cannot be spared, there is little to be known about the quality of statistics beyond common-sense 'hunches' incapable of expression in quantitative measures. If this defence is to be accepted, then the value of much of the current use of economic statistics as a foundation for policy is in doubt. As we have shown, this use often depends on differences between two quantities, and if these quantities are both subject to substantial but quite unknown errors their difference will indeed be an unsure foundation. We do not underestimate the difficulty of assessing accuracy or quality, but we suggest that the subject is so important that it needs more attention, even if as a result the output of statistics has to be reduced. We have found a few cases where factors which *prima facie* would seem obvious sources of bias have been neglected; this seems to us to be symptomatic of a general failure to give sufficient attention to quality.

The problem of accuracy has recently received some attention in America in connexion with the construction of input-output tables and the applications of linear programming. Professor Morgenstern's condemnation is forthright:[1]

'Yet, it ought to be clear *a priori* that most economic statistics should not be reported at all in the manner in which they are frequently encountered. Changes in consumers' total spending power are reported, and taken seriously, down to the last billion (i.e., about one-half per-cent!), price indexes for wholesale prices are shown to second decimals, when there have been so many computing steps that the rounding off errors alone may obliterate such a degree of precision. Unemployment figures of several millions are given down to the last 1,000's (i.e., one-tenth of one percent accuracy!), when even the 100,000's or the millions are in doubt. All this is stated without any reference whatsoever to the error of observation. It will be seen later that national income and consumers' spending power probably cannot be known now without an error of ± 15 to ± 20 percent.'

Here, and elsewhere in his monograph, Professor Morgenstern seems to us to overstate his case, even in relation to the American statistics which he mentions. But the case is a strong one, and the monograph does a valuable service in analysing the different forms which error may take in economic statistics. We will now attempt a similar discussion ourselves, relating it to what we have discovered about British statistics.

FACTORS AFFECTING QUALITY: (I) DIVERSION TO ANOTHER USE

Occasionally a piece of economic information is produced by a 'designed experiment'—that is to say, by a special investigation, undertaken solely in order to produce the information desired, and therefore designed to yield the facts in just the form which their final user requires. An example is the special sample investigation of capital expenditure in manufacturing industry in 1948 and 1949, which provided information for the then National Income White Paper's estimates of gross capital formation.[2] But such instances are rare. Sometimes information comes from a general inquiry, or census, which, being designed to assist different kinds of user, suits none of them exactly. The special investigation mentioned above was additional to Censuses of Production covering the same field, since these Censuses did not at that time yield estimates of capital formation at the time and in the form required by the White Paper.[3] It was therefore necessary to ask sample firms, which had

---

[1] [107], p. 6.   [2] [34a], pp. 45 and 76: *Board of Trade Journal* [12], 21 April 1951.
[3] The estimates are now, however, based on a special advance analysis of Census data.

already answered questions about their purchases during the year, to give the information again in a different form.

But for the most part economic statistics are produced as a by-product of administration, and much of the statistician's skill is employed in diverting the streams of administrative data and using them in his own ways. This is particularly obvious in dealing with economic aggregates which are found as a by-product of the collection of revenue. The estimate of 'rent of land and buildings'[1] is, of course, not what the theorist would call 'economic rent'; but neither is it the sum of the cash payments made as what is in common parlance called 'rent'. It is, for the most part, an excess of house rents 'received' over insurance and repairs, together with the interest on local authority housing debt, and Schedule A net assessments for business premises. Its relation to actual rent payments depends on the care taken in determining or adjusting Schedule A assessments, on local authority rent policy, and so on. Again, 'depreciation'[2] is not an estimate of the actual depreciation of capital made during the year, nor is it the sum of financial provisions actually made to meet depreciation; it is a hybrid concept, composed in part of allowances made for tax purposes, in part of financial provisions made, and in part of estimates of actual depreciation.

In both these cases the statistician has to do the best he can with the data available from the Inland Revenue Department, and his estimates may be subjected to alteration because of some quite unrelated changes in tax policy. Such changes were the grant, increase, subsequent withdrawal, and return of 'initial allowances' on capital expenditure, which have altered the way in which the allowance for depreciation (already in part arbitrary) is distributed over the years. Statistics of the share in the national income of the various 'factors of production', which are of considerable economic interest, will also be found to be based mainly on the tax Schedules; consequently definitions (for example of trading profits) are those found convenient for tax purposes, and may diverge in important ways from those used by economists.

This use of statistics obtained for administrative purposes to illuminate quite different fields will be found to be very frequent. Thus, the food consumption statistics, important both as a large constituent of the estimates of consumers' expenditure and in relation to nutritional needs, are a by-product of the Ministry of Food's rationing and other controls. Supplies of utility furniture were known because of the existence of the utility scheme. The dismantling of clothes rationing has made it more difficult to follow the flow of clothing to the home market, since reliance must now be placed on wholesale and retail trade statistics in value terms. In fact, a large part of the extra statistical knowledge which has

[1] [34c], p. 56.   [2] [34c], p. 85.

become available in Britain since 1938 is a by-product of wartime controls. Some of it has been lost with the dismantling of the controls; much more continues an insecure existence, having lost its original justification, and being carried on either by the voluntary goodwill of firms or under special powers. Building and civil engineering statistics, for instance, rest on returns from registered contractors collected under Defence Regulation 56 AB.

There is little that can be done to lessen this dependence of the statistician on material provided by the administrator; it is usually obvious common sense, and the alternative, to collect the information by separate and direct inquiry, would be (even if possible) far too expensive. We have no recommendations to make, but we hope that, by drawing attention to the problem, we may help to promote two tendencies. One is for the administrator to regard the statistician, not as an accidental user of the data collected in administration, but as an important colleague who ought to be brought into consultation. Small changes in the method of collecting data may greatly improve their value as economic statistics; and a few moments' consultation can help to avoid those irritating discontinuities in data which arise from administrative decisions taken without regard to the statistical by-product. We are encouraged to find evidence that such consultation does in fact often take place, but we think that the statisticians' hands deserve to be further strengthened. They may reasonably ask, too, for facilities for filling in (perhaps by sampling studies) gaps which the accidents of administration leave in official statistics.

The second tendency which we note with approval, but think might go further, is for statisticians to be scrupulous in drawing attention to 'diversions' of administrative data which do not give a perfect fit to the statistical needs. There is a job in public relations to be done here, which is too often left to an obscure footnote. The national income estimates, for instance, are widely used by people who are not experts; and we are glad to see the marked improvement shown by the 1952 Blue Book in the explanations given of the way in which the items are built up. But there is still more to be done before the casual user will realize that special meanings have to be given to words such as 'profit', 'depreciation', 'wage' and 'rent'.

FACTORS AFFECTING QUALITY: (II) IMPERFECTIONS
IN THE MATERIAL

The problem which we have just discussed is the problem of dressing ideas in a statistical suit of clothes which does not quite fit them. We now have to consider the possibility that the suit may be made of poor-quality cloth.

The possibilities of poor quality in the basic statistics are numerous. There may be a deliberate attempt, on the part of those who have to make statistical returns, to withhold information or to distort it. The chances of this can usually be surmised by considering whether any disadvantage would follow, or could by ignorant people be supposed to follow, from telling the truth. Thus, any information based on tax returns is suspect, since it is certain that some taxpayers escape the net of the Inland Revenue and Customs and Excise Departments, while others understate their income, or the value of dutiable goods. In a time of labour shortage, employers will tend to distort labour returns so as to give an impression of the high priority of their work. Returns of labour engaged on export work are probably biased upwards in this way. Despite a comprehensive system of national insurance, the occupied population certainly exceeds the insured population plus those known to be legally non-insured though occupied, for there is an obvious temptation to evade the payment of contributions. An industrialist may understate his stock of some commodity in short supply, if he fears that a true statement will result in his being refused further deliveries until his stock has been reduced. Some forms of concealment are considered proper and respectable; thus, the balance sheets of the banks withhold information which might seem essential to the shareholders.

It is probable that not very much concealment or falsehood arises from people deliberately writing down a figure which they know to be wholly imaginary. It arises much more frequently from some uncertainty or ambiguity, real or imagined, in the request for information—the respondent interpreting the request in a manner which is to his advantage. Which of us, asked for a return of expenses 'wholly, necessarily and exclusively' incurred in the course of business, does not cast about for extra items to include? A badly designed questionnaire can, by the ambiguity of its questions, produce incorrect results even in the absence of an incentive to choose one interpretation, but there is then a fair chance that the individual errors will cancel each other out in the aggregate. A choice of interpretations becomes far more dangerous when there is an incentive—however slight—to choose a particular one.

Another form of concealment is worth mentioning: the attitude of the person questioned may make it impossible to ask him for some types of information with any hope of success. Thus, in some trades there is no 'market price', but a complex of different prices and discounts for different buyers—prices which must be kept as trade secrets. Some industries refuse to collect or to publish statistics of output or sales (except such as are legally required under the Statistics of Trade Act); individual firms are obsessed by the fear that their competitors will learn about their position. Questions about what people think, or what they would do in some hypothetical situation, or even what they will do next year, may run up against unexpected obstacles in the respondent's mind, and he will answer what he thinks he is expected to answer instead of giving his own considered judgement.

Another large class of errors is brought in when we consider those due to the ignorance or the laziness of informants. A distinction can be made between statistical information which should already exist in the records of the respondent—for example returns of income, production, sales, numbers employed—and information which has to be 'got out' specially. An example can be seen on the monthly site return made by building contractors to the Ministry of Works. This asks for the number of men employed on the last pay-day of the month—a figure which the employer should be able to give accurately. It also asks for the estimated value of work completed (including overheads and profit), and for the percentage of the contract completed to date. The average building contractor takes a fair time to cost a job even when he has finished it, and he will not (if he is a small man) have any records which will enable him to quote a value for a given month. Presumably, therefore, he will guess—probably using as a guide the licensed value of the building. These site returns are fundamental to the building statistics, and their use implies a good deal of faith in the propensity of guesses to add up into unbiased estimates.

Sometimes, statistical returns may be biased because the population from which they are drawn has not been fully enumerated. The building statistics again provide a possible example, though their quality seems to be reasonably good. Quarterly returns are made by a sample of registered building and civil engineering contractors, and the register is maintained under powers given by Defence Regulation 56AB. Will an unemployed building operative who decides to do small jobs on his own account for a few months know about this register? It will be easy for him to suppose that such controls are for larger businesses, and the trouble of finding out his true position will not be outweighed by the danger of a small fine. He may also have an ignorant fear that the register is something to do with income tax. There will in fact be a general presumption that small firms will be under-represented in statistical returns because they have not been discovered, as well as because they often fail to respond.

Failure to obtain a large enough percentage of response is another difficulty which not only gives rise to error, but also delays the production of statistics while the stragglers are being chased. The danger of error arises in 'grossing up' an incomplete return to take account of the missing members, for there may be a correlation between the propensity to respond and the characteristic being investigated. It is sometimes possible to deal with this by investigating early and late responses separately, or by following up a sample of non-respondents by personal calls, in order to find out whether such a correlation exists. But it may be more efficient to spend one's limited resources on obtaining a full response from a sample, rather than an incomplete response from the whole population.

This discussion of sources of error leads directly to our main conclusion in this field: namely, that the possibilities of error in British economic statistics are too little discussed. In consequence, experiments designed to establish the nature and size of errors are too few; users of statistics are left largely in doubt about the quality of the material which they are using; and (in particular) the possibility of instability in an estimate, owing to its being derived from other statistics whose errors are correlated, has received hardly any attention at all. Many of the statisticians we have consulted have seemed well satisfied with the quality of their own figures even though there would seem *a priori* to be reason to suspect bias; but this confidence has seemed to be based on a subjective 'hunch' rather than on any thorough investigation. In saying this, we are not making any general condemnation of the quality of British economic statistics—which is usually high; nor do we underestimate the value of the 'hunch', which may (indeed) be the only judgement of quality possible. But we think that, in the long run, British statistics would gain both in usefulness and in public respect if there were explicit acknowledgement and discussion of errors. We put forward the following suggestions:

(i) Where a suspected bias is corrected, the correction should be explicitly stated, so that it will be open to further investigation and criticism. The National Income Blue Book, for instance, must make some assumptions about the size of tax evasion. It is true that this is wrapped up in an estimate subject to other errors, and it is not easy to separate it; but it is an important figure, which should either be shown or at least be mentioned.

(ii) Important statistics should have attached to them some discussion of the errors to which, *a priori*, they would seem likely to be subject. Often these errors are only known by the statistician who prepares the figures, and later users may be misled by a spurious appearance of accuracy.

(iii) More resources should be devoted to sample investigations of error—for example an investigation of the completeness of a register in a particular area.

(iv) Subjective estimates of error (for example grouping of estimates into classes according to their quality) should be made whenever quantitative investigations are impossible, and these subjective estimates should be published. An example of this form of treatment can be found in Chapter XVI of *Wages and Salaries in the United Kingdom, 1920–1938*, by Miss Agatha L. Chapman.[1] Miss Chapman divides her figures into four classes:

A	'Firm figures'	(probability $\geqslant 95\%$ that error $<\ 5\%$)
B	'Good estimates'	(probability $\geqslant 95\%$ that error $< 10\%$)
C	'Rough estimates'	(probability $\geqslant 95\%$ that error $< 25\%$)
D	'Conjectures'	(the rest)

In some types of work the assignment of figures to these classes would be wholly subjective, but Miss Chapman develops rule-of-thumb methods; thus, if the number employed in an industry is given by the Census of Population as x and by the Census of Production as y, she classes the error as $\frac{1}{2}(x-y)$. She also discusses the interrelation of her errors, and the effect of given errors in earnings and numbers employed on the estimate of a total wage bill. The whole chapter provides an admirable example of the kind of technique which we should like to see widely applied.

FACTORS AFFECTING QUALITY: (III) EFFECTS OF PROCESSING

We have considered the possibilities that statistics may be of poor material, or ill-suited to their purpose; but there is the further possibility, that they acquire error in the course of processing. For the sake of completeness, one may include in this group errors of sampling, since they are in a sense introduced by a deliberate decision of the statistician; but sampling errors have received far more attention than other types, and it is rare for them to be ignored in a sample investigation. We will not, therefore, discuss them further.

The important processing errors are of two kinds. One is the arithmetical error, arising in the course of computation; but it is usually possible to design scientific checking procedures which will keep this within bounds. An allied form of error is that due to the use of rounded data. Statisticians are much too frightened of 'spurious accuracy'— that is to say, of quoting more 'significant' figures than the quality of the data will justify. As we have seen above, this fault is severely condemned by Professor Morgenstern,[2] but his condemnation seems to us to be misdirected. What is wrong is the giving of estimates, apparently highly accurate, *without any reference to their errors*. But the premature rounding of figures which are likely to be subjected to further arithmetical processes is a great nuisance. It is not logically justified: if the enumerated population of an area is 5,621,723 this should be given as the best estimate available, even though a footnote may draw attention to the fact that no confidence can be placed in the last three figures. For it remains true that 5,621,723 is a better estimate, on the information available, than 5,622,000.

The other class of error which can arise in processing is that due to the need to fill in missing bits of data. This is very obvious in world economic statistics, because of the slowness or uncertainty of information from some areas; estimates of the world wheat crop, for instance, often contain 'dummy' figures for the U.S.S.R. and China. But the difficulty is a very general one; many of the series in the National Income Blue Book, for instance, are not available for the latest year at the time of publication, and consequently must be extrapolated from past data, estimated on partial information, or just guessed. This filling in of gaps is quite inevitable if statistics are to be ready in time to meet the needs of the policy-maker. In line with our previous recommendations, however, we feel that more should be done to show which estimates are especially 'provisional' because vital facts are missing, and to give some idea of the way in which these provisional estimates have been obtained.

It would not be fair to leave this subject without pointing out that the National Income Blue Book presents special difficulties; for it consists of a system of accounts which have to be adjusted to obtain consistency. The raw material therefore goes through a very complicated process before the final estimates are reached, and these final estimates may (because they are consistent parts of the whole) be much more reliable than a discussion of possible errors would suggest. On the other hand, the errors on two sides of an account may be correlated, giving a sort of spurious consistency. For this reason we should especially welcome a study of quality in relation to the Blue Book, including an investigation of the proper way of adjusting its figures, with their varying accuracy, to achieve consistency.

DIFFICULTIES IN THE PURSUIT OF QUALITY

It will already have become apparent that the pursuit of quality involves trouble and expense—so that it becomes necessary to decide whether to have fewer statistics in order that they may be better. But this is not the only dilemma. We have seen how it may be necessary to use statistics which are by-products of administration, and which do not precisely fit the concepts being studied. Occasionally it may be possible to alter administrative processes and to improve the fit; but this will break the continuity of the existing series. What weight should be given to continuity?

A break in continuity is a single inconvenience, though often a great one; a bad time-series is a continuing evil. It therefore seems to us that the virtues of continuity may tend to be overrated. If the change to a better series must in any case come in time, there will usually be no advantage in waiting. Continuity should carry the day only if the bad series can be tolerated indefinitely. But, of course, the best solution is to give some thought to the design of a 'bridge' between the old series and the new. Unfortunately, where large changes are involved this may itself be an expensive operation; though not enough has been done to provide 'bridges' over some recent breaks in series.

Another dilemma is that of speed of publication versus accuracy; but this is only part of the general problem of speed of publication, which we shall discuss below.[1] We have already illustrated it in relation to the National Income Blue Book, which would be at least two years later than it is if it waited for the last firm figure to arrive. Yet another problem, of increasing importance, is created by the pressure (felt through the various international agencies) for international comparability of statistics. Definitions which suit an 'average' country may be less suited to the special conditions of Britain than those which we at present employ. It will often be possible to secure international comparability while preserving both the continuity and the quality of existing series; but this again may be expensive.

CONCLUSION

It has been our purpose in this chapter to give some idea of the difficulty and complexity of the problem of securing a good standard of quality in economic statistics. It is a problem which, as we have mentioned at several points, needs more explicit attention—in acknowledging known sources of error, in drawing attention to possible sources, and in studying their habits and relations. Most official statisticians are too much burdened by day-to-day work to give the matter the attention it needs, unless it can be given a higher priority. We hope it will obtain that priority, and that there will also be research by non-official investigators. The 'efficiency studies' which we shall propose in Chapter XII are needed in this field also, for accuracy is often slow and expensive. The methods of collection and handling of statistics need to be designed so as to yield the right combination of quality with speed and cheapness; this is a matter which deserves more general and theoretical study, in addition to the piecemeal investigation of practical problems.

[1] P. 135.

CHAPTER XI

THE PRESENTATION AND AVAILABILITY OF STATISTICS

This chapter will consider the way in which statistical information is offered to the public. This requires first that we should look at the kind of people who use such knowledge, and assess their needs. Then we shall examine the present practice in this country with respect to both the presentation and the availability of official statistics. Lastly we shall offer some suggestions for improvement.

It is clear that, while the Government policy-maker is an important consumer of statistics, he is not, strictly speaking, a member of the statistical public. His position is a privileged one and he can make use within limits of any knowledge existing within the civil service. He can ask in principle as many questions as he likes about the sources and reliability of the information offered to him. If necessary he can insist that a special investigation be conducted to provide further knowledge, for example a sampling inquiry by the Social Survey.

The public, whose needs are to be considered here, cannot make their requirements so easily known in official statistical quarters. Although the statistical public is not large numerically, it has important functions to fulfil. The main types of these users of statistics in the world outside the civil service have been enumerated earlier in this report.[1] There they were called the 'general' and the 'business' users, and the economic historians can be distinguished as a separate class. Here we consider their needs in rather more detail.

The 'general users' include those professional economists in academic life, city editors, financial journalists and intelligence officers of firms and other bodies who make it their business to criticize and appraise the policy decisions of the Government of the day. They include, too, those politicians who are not at the moment in the fortunate position of having direct access to official information, that is, the opposition front bench and the back-benchers of all parties. Anyone, indeed, who might describe himself as a student of affairs, with a particular interest in their economic aspects, can be included under this broad heading. None of these people can afford to assume that the official interpretation of a problem or the decisions taken to deal with it are necessarily correct or reasonable. Thus, in so far as such disclosures are not unreasonably expensive or inconsistent with public safety, they would like access to

[1] Chapter II, pp. 13–15.

much of the official information that bears upon the question under consideration. They can then make an independent study of the situation disclosed and assess for themselves the adequacy or relevance of Governmental proposals or actions.

The outside users will want, for instance, estimates and forecasts of such aggregates as the national income, investment, and consumption expenditure and details of the balance of payments, and also in certain cases the crude data on which such estimates are based. They will want to get their information without undue delay, so that their contributions to public discussion can be of practical value.

The 'business users' include professional economists and statisticians, accountants, representatives of Trade Unions and Employers' Associations, and others who are employed in industry and commerce; anyone, in fact, who is interested in economic information in order to serve the company or firm for which he works. Such people's interests are likely to be more specialized. General economic problems will only be relevant so far as they directly affect the fortunes of the particular business concerned. Thus while the effects of, say, budgetary policy on the demand for a company's products or on the profits that it can distribute are not matters of indifference, there is very much else besides on which the business user will want adequate and frequent enlightenment. The total production of the raw materials that the firm uses is of considerable interest; so too are the movements in the stocks of these commodities and their prices in the various possible markets in which they might be bought. The level of output of the industry of which the firm is part will enable the business man to see how his firm's output relates to that of the industry as a whole. Detailed international trade statistics will reveal the industry's export trade, and the countries in which such exports are expanding or stationary. In general the experience of a single unit of production can be compared with the industry's fortunes, and the differences noted and examined.

Now that more and more attention is being given to the inadequacy of conventional depreciation allowances for capital equipment in times of rapidly changing prices, the business man will need detailed information about the prices of the sort of equipment used by his firm. Labour troubles may be avoided or moderated if adequate and timely knowledge is obtained about wage rates and earnings in similar occupations, about the cost of travel to or from work, or about the movements in the level of retail prices, and as the business users are advisers to, or are themselves, men who must take decisions, they require their information to be as timely as that for the general users.

The economic historians are a third category of users of official statistics. The members of this group are sharply distinguished from the other two because, instead of being concerned with what is happening now or is likely to occur in the near future, they are interested in discovering *why* things happened in the past. Thus the literary historian and the builder of statistical models of the economic system are yoke-fellows. Both in their different ways have a theory about the unfolding of past events; both are concerned to see if the existing evidence is consistent with their theories.

It may be tempting for men of action to decry the value of these activities and to suggest that the pure theorists be left to scavenge for their materials as best they may. But if the connexion between today's actions and the testing of new economic theories appears somewhat remote, there can be no doubt about its existence. No policy can be formulated or criticized in the absence of a theory about the mode of operation of the economic system. The more adequate the supporting theory, the more successful, other things being equal, will be the policy which derives from it. Someone must, however, be charged with the job of reviewing the currently held theory in the light of the new knowledge which the passage of time yields. Inconsistencies so revealed enable the necessary modifications to be made to the present theory. Thus the economic historians use statistical information in order that men may learn from experience and avoid repeating the same errors of judgement.

Prompt publication of information is certainly not of first importance to these workers. Their greatest need is for long runs of statistical series, with comprehensive accounts of the methods of compilation and of the errors and other limitations to which they are subject.

It should not be forgotten that there is also a non-technical public for certain kinds of statistical information. It is extremely desirable that important economic problems should excite general and not only expert interest. Indeed politicians are often more concerned about popular reaction to their decisions than about the opinions of the well-informed. The popularization of economic information requires considerable skill, if attempts to reach the masses are not to avoid technicalities only at the expense of falsifying the important questions at issue. The honest politician will seek to educate his masters honestly.

PRESENT STANDARDS OF STATISTICAL INFORMATION

What sort of statistical information service is offered by Government statisticians to the clientele described above? It is convenient to discuss the present qualities of this service from two different points of view: first the manner of presentation of information, and secondly its availability, whether by publication or otherwise.

The first releases of current statistics are often in the form of regular duplicated hand-outs to the press and to certain specially interested individuals. This is true, for example, of the weekly information about coal output and stocks, the Ministry of Labour's monthly analysis of the employment position, and the Board of Trade's statistics of retail sales.

A wider public is reached at a later stage when the same figures are published in the monthly journals or statistical bulletins of the department or public corporation concerned. Thus the National Coal Board produces monthly its *Coal Figures*[1] and the Ministry of Labour the *Ministry of Labour Gazette*. In some fields, however, the preliminary hand-out does not take place and the first notification is received when, for example, the Board of Trade publishes in the *Board of Trade Journal* monthly figures of the output of cloth and yarn for the various parts of the textile industry, or quarterly estimates of the volume and average values of imports and exports. The British Transport Commission combines both stages at once; its monthly bulletin *Transport Statistics*, while giving a full range of figures up to and including a particular four-week period, includes a detached printed slip giving a few selected figures for the following period.

Other statistics are presented by means of Government papers printed at regular intervals. This is true of statistical information which is in essence derived indirectly from basic statistics. Important examples are the annual National Income Blue Book (formerly a White Paper) and the twice-yearly Balance of Payments White Paper.

Many annual reports of Government departments or of nationalized industries, although not always primarily of a statistical character, include statistical sections. Examples of this method of presentation are the Annual Reports of the Commissioners of Inland Revenue, the Annual Report of the Ministry of Education, the annual publication called *The Colonial Territories*, and the Annual Reports and Accounts of the National Coal Board and of the British Transport Commission.

The Central Statistical Office itself performs an important function in the compilation of two purely statistical publications which contain information drawn from a wide variety of official and other sources. The *Monthly Digest of Statistics*, which has been published since January 1946, contains information some of which has already been published in such places as the *Ministry of Labour Gazette* and the *Board of Trade Journal* but much of which sees the light of day for the first time. The *Annual Abstract of Statistics* provides the statistician with an even more comprehensive range of information compiled upon a yearly basis.

The *Monthly Digest of Statistics*, non-existent before the Second World War, has proved itself invaluable to everyone with statistical interests.

[1] Discontinued 1953.

The *Annual Abstract of Statistics*, although now more comprehensive, more attractively laid out and better printed, is in fact the continuation of a series of which no less than eighty-three numbers were printed between 1854 and 1940.[1]

The regular issue of these two publications of very high quality represents an important technical advance in the presentation of official statistics. Nevertheless there still exist certain irritants to the regular user of these sources of information. The costs of and the time taken in printing necessarily impose a severe limitation on the size of such publications. The Central Statistical Office has to decide what to print; such selection can take place in various different (but not mutually exclusive) ways. Particular series of figures can be excluded; the series selected can be published for a limited number of months or years only; the notes and explanations attached to each series or table can be reduced to a minimum.

In practice all the methods mentioned have had perforce to be adopted. The detail given for a particular field of statistics is often less complete in the *Digest* and *Abstract* than in the parent publication from which the figures were drawn. This means that the user may often after a preliminary examination of the *Digest* be forced to consult the *Ministry of Labour Gazette* or the *Board of Trade Journal* or even, as in the case of the Post Office Savings Bank returns, the *London Gazette*. In the *Monthly Digest of Statistics* the run of the monthly figures is comparatively short (usually about 25 months) and annual figures are given for four or five recent years and sometimes a similar number of pre-war years.[2] The *Annual Abstract of Statistics* contains data for a continuous period not usually exceeding 10–12 years. The user who seeks a really long run for a particular series must often dig them out himself from a number of separate publications. The privately run *Bulletin* of the London and Cambridge Economic Service [124] is virtually alone among statistical publications in trying to provide continuous series over a period of about thirty years.

The explanatory notes to the *Monthly Digest of Statistics* are published separately in a pamphlet which is revised and brought up to date annually, but even so many of the necessary qualifications that a conscientious user requires to know can only be discovered by referring to

---

[1] Another post-war advance is the monthly *Report on Overseas Trade* [43], which saves the regular user of foreign trade statistics much weary work in analysing the Trade and Navigation Accounts.

[2] The *Monthly Digest of Statistics* in July 1953 contained 129 pages of tables (156 different tables in all). There are between 1,600 and 2,000 different series on a monthly or quarterly basis.

The United States Department of Commerce's *Survey of Current Business* contains, apart from articles, forty pages of monthly statistics with a run of thirteen months. The total number of series given is between 2,500 and 3,000.

the original source, for example the *Board of Trade Journal*. Even here the answer may only be found by working back through the volumes until an explanatory article accompanying the very first issue of the series is uncovered. The *Annual Abstract of Statistics* loses a significant part of its value as a work of reference because it is accompanied by hardly any adequate explanatory notes, but simply by a list of the main sources from which the series and other information were derived. This deficiency makes the problem of obtaining a long run of figures, to which reference has already been made, often insuperable in the short run, since it may not be possible to discover the differences in definition between post-war and pre-war series with similar titles without making special enquiries at the Government departments concerned. For some series no continuous run exists; thus indices of import and export volumes and average values and of retail prices have a break when the weights used for computation are changed. The user may therefore have to splice together separate bits of series on his own, without aid from the official statisticians.

So far any criticism of the method of presenting statistics has measured the official statisticians' success in terms of the aims which they themselves have apparently set. Their publications are directed mainly towards the technical expert in the field of economic statistics. Now even the members of the statistical public enumerated in the first section of this chapter would hardly claim to possess a high degree of competence over the whole statistical field. An intelligent industrial statistician or business man, who knows the ropes so far as the prices and stock movements of his own especial commodities are concerned, could hardly be blamed if he were at sea with national income or balance of payments statistics. The same remarks may well apply to the academic expert on, say, labour statistics.

Thus a substantial proportion of the statistical public and all the lay public must rely for the interpretation of statistics of national income and of the balance of payments on the unofficial comment of city editors, financial journalists, and others. Occasionally a Ministerial statement in Parliament may also shed light on what was otherwise obscure. Apart from this, official comment is restricted to a few pages in the annual *Economic Survey*, which itself is a highly technical document. It is true that it has become the custom to publish a popular version of the *Economic Survey*, but in fact the result has been a pamphlet which verges on the trivial.

There is clearly a need for presenting certain important statistics in a form that enables their import to be easily digested by the intelligent non-technician. In such official publications, great masses of figures can be replaced by simple verbal explanations, charts and diagrams. The

United States Department of Commerce's *Survey of Current Business* provides many excellent examples of what can be done by this means. Quite apart from the educational value of important economic facts thus presented, business men may be persuaded that the information which many of them rather reluctantly provide is in fact used to help them understand what is going on in the economy in which they function.

There is also a very good case for allowing members of the civil service to write articles on topics of current but not necessarily lasting interest, addressed to the general reader. It might be necessary to create a new publication for this purpose, but there appears to be little reason why both the *Board of Trade Journal* and the *Ministry of Labour Gazette* should not be partially adapted to meet this need. The preservation of the anonymity of officials is perhaps carried to excessive lengths, and if such articles bore the name of their author not only would the Government be less committed in the minds of the public to the personal views expressed, but also the writers themselves would find such a practice both helpful and encouraging as their reputations were widened and enhanced. Members of the so-called scientific departments are already allowed to express themselves in this way, and there is little logic in treating civil servants concerned with economic affairs on an entirely different footing.

In the case of what may be called 'derived official statistics', for example balance of payments statistics, the presentation is not adequate even from the point of view of the unofficial expert. The technical notes that are provided refer in the main to definitions rather than to the devices employed in the compilation and to the possible errors that may result. In default of such information it is very easy to attribute an undue significance to small variations over time in particular estimates, and it is at the same time very difficult to make private forecasts of future movements in important aggregates of transactions. At present notes to tables of estimates do not draw attention to abnormal movements of a purely statistical character. For example, the lifting of restrictions on the sale of second-hand ships abroad caused a fall, other things being equal, in capital formation since the transactions involved are regarded as negative capital formation. Detailed published studies are, therefore, required to keep the technician fully informed about official methods of estimation.[1]

No doubt the series of pamphlets entitled *Studies in Official Statistics* was originally intended to fill this gap, but as it happens only two pamphlets have reached the public.[2] In fairness, perhaps, the official description of the interim index of retail prices could also be regarded

---

[1] For an American example, see *National Income, 1929–1950* [74].
[2] [62] and [62a], both on indices of industrial production.

as belonging to the same stable, although it was published as a supplement to the Ministry of Labour's *Industrial Relations Handbook*.[1] At the moment detailed knowledge can only be acquired by private approaches to Government departments, or by consulting articles contributed to the *Journal of the Royal Statistical Society*.[2]

Nowhere can be found anything, official or unofficial, that deals adequately with the size and character of the errors in official estimates. This fact has already been mentioned with great frequency in earlier chapters, but is worth repeating here as a fault in presentation. Government White Papers themselves contain only such comments as 'The paucity of information on the extent and nature of changes in the value of stocks renders the estimates...highly precarious',[3] or 'The direct information...is so scanty...that the figure remains subject to a very wide margin of error'.[4] If the figures referred to are to be employed intelligently, much more information than this must be given.[5]

This would seem to be the right place to emphasize that some general idea of the method of compilation and of the reliability of derived official statistics should be given in popular presentations of statistics to the ordinary public. The implications of movements in an index of production for a particular industry or for manufacturing industry as a whole cannot be appreciated without at least an inkling of the way that the raw statistical material is assembled. Thus it is important to distinguish between those who want to know the finer details of the construction, that is the experts, and those who need only the general principles to be explained, but who will be almost certain to misinterpret the figures if such principles are not fully understood.

AVAILABILITY

The subject of the 'availability' of official statistics can be split into two parts. There is first of all the degree to which statistical information collected by Government agencies is accessible to the general public, and secondly the speed with which the statistics selected for periodical publication reach potential users.

It has already been mentioned that both the costs of printing and consideration of time taken must inevitably impose a limit on the amount of information that can be regularly published. In addition many figures cannot be released at all (or not in fine detail) because of the

---

[1] [64]. This was later reissued as *Interim Index of Retail Prices: Method of Construction and Calculation*. See also *Report on the Working of the Index of Retail Prices* [63].

[2] Some are reprinted in Kendall [102]: a second volume is in prospect.

[3] See Cmd. 8203 [34a], p. 55.   [4] Ibid. p. 4.

[5] The national income statisticians of the Irish Republic showed initiative in this field but seem to have suffered a relapse.

necessity to preserve confidentiality. This reason covers the withholding of information in the interests of national security, to maintain Parliamentary privilege, or to avoid the disclosure of the affairs of individual companies and persons. Only the last will be discussed in what follows.

It would be irresponsible to suggest that the preservation of confidentiality for reasons other than that of national security is unnecessary. Nevertheless there exists a tendency to interpret the statutory requirements of the Statistics of Trade Act rather too narrowly on occasions. Even within the civil service itself a ministerial direction is required before the Direct Employment ('L') Returns of the Ministry of Labour may be consulted by other departments. Workers on the distribution of industry in the Board of Trade cannot obtain access to the original returns submitted for the Census of Production to the same department.

Many documents, which clearly must remain confidential in the form that is originally needed for an administrative process, could be rendered quite harmless by the subsequent detachment of certain details or of the identification of the informant, or both. The Pay-As-You-Earn Income Tax forms, which are at present lost for ever in the office of the Board of Inland Revenue, would yield invaluable information about labour movement and turnover if such an adaptation could be made. Since the entries on those forms are subject to the stringent financial check of accounting for the tax collected, the statistics derived from them would be of unrivalled reliability.

The members of the Interdepartmental Committee on Social and Economic Research (the North Committee) have given considerable thought to the problem of confidentiality, these being some of their observations:

'It is neither possible nor desirable to evolve a legal form of words defining the limits of confidentiality. Each [Government] Department must necessarily exercise its own discretion with a full sense of its responsibility to the requirements of Government and the needs of the community as a whole. It is a recognized duty of Departments towards the society of which they are the institutional agents to make available, at least for the purposes of scientific enquiry, as much as possible of the information which they possess. In our opinion a *prima facie* case exists for publishing, or making otherwise accessible, all information of general social utility, unless there is good reason to the contrary.

'It is necessary to examine what constitutes a good reason to the contrary.

'In the first place, statutory requirements must be faithfully observed. At the same time we hope that Departments may take opportunities provided in the course of amending legislation to ask Parliament to modify them, e.g., in cases where they have become obsolete.

'Secondly, the requirements of security and public policy must be met.... We ask Departments to interpret the rules applying to them as liberally as possible and to review their classification of documents so that information may be made available to research workers without undue delay.

'Thirdly, the practical administration of Departments must not be hampered. On the other hand the argument of Departmental inconvenience should not be pressed too far.

'Fourthly, the cost should not be out of proportion to the importance of the subject matter. The question of cost arises when an enquiry involves tabulation, analysis or preparing material in other ways.... Departments must obviously protect themselves against unreasonable requests. On the other hand if scientists of good standing consider that certain information is important, though from a Departmental point of view it seems trivial, we consider that every effort should be made to make it available.

'Fifthly, public interest demands that the obligation, whether statutory or otherwise, to ensure that individual persons, firms and other entities are not publicly identifiable must be discharged. This can often be met merely by refraining from identifying the returns, as is done for example in most family budget investigations, or by using a method of aggregation such as the "rule of three" adopted by the Board of Trade. Public interest equally requires that Departments, having discharged their duty of protecting individuals, should make available as much as possible of the information in aggregate form....

'There is another type of material...namely, information which Departments obtain for administrative purposes from such bodies as Trade Unions, Employers' Federations, and Trade and Professional Associations, but not by means of statutory or voluntary returns.... Such documents might possibly, however, be subject to a process of scheduling, analogous to the scheduling for purposes of destruction and preservation that now takes place for ordinary Department documents [see p. 134 of this chapter], and we suggest that Departments should consider whether they could, after consultation with the appropriate bodies, set time limits to the inaccessibility of material of this nature so that on the expiry of a given time period it may be made available to research workers....

'The same sort of time-limit might well be set on certain confidential Departmental material. In some cases no provision whatsoever is made for the eventual release of information....'[1]

The satisfactory treatment of the problem of confidentiality also requires the formulation of a long-term policy. The forms on which

[1] [65a], pp. 9, 10.

returns are rendered need to be examined to determine whether the passage of time alone is sufficient to remove the ban on publication or whether the forms used can be suitably altered so that confidentiality can be more easily preserved. Although a promise of confidentiality should never be abused, it is most undesirable that it should be given too easily. The bias of policy should be towards open returns unless there is proven necessity to the contrary.

Unfortunately the anxiety of the Government to allay suspicions of business men about the Statistics of Trade Bill caused unduly stringent provisions to be incorporated in the Act. This has meant that the lapsing of defence regulations has often had the effect of rendering inaccessible information which had previously been made available for years without causing an outcry, for example the 'L' returns. It is unfortunate if a Government is so sensitive to unreasonable demands from business men that innocuous material lies hid for ever.

Bound up to some extent with the preservation of secrecy is official policy over the destruction of old files and documents. There is clearly a temptation to discard such possessions when they have ceased to serve a useful official function. It cannot be so certain, however, when the time arrives, that such records are of no potential value to academic economists or historians. The North Committee has spent some of its time considering the existing procedure and has reported as follows:

'...The position is that, under the Public Record Office Acts of 1887 and 1898, Departments are required to preserve all documents except those belonging to specified classes which, as shown in Schedules approved under the Acts in respect of each Department, may be destroyed without delay or after the lapse of a prescribed interval. As an additional safeguard it is usual for the Schedules, which are prepared by representatives of the Departments concerned and Inspecting Officers of the Public Record Office, to contain a clause to the effect that documents to be destroyed "will first be examined by a competent officer, who will withdraw for preservation any documents containing matter likely to be of value as a precedent or to be of historical or legal importance". Following acceptance by the Public Record Office of a recommendation made in our first Report [Cmd. 7537], the words "or useful for social and economic research" are being added to this clause.

'...we have recently asked Departments...to look into current practice in order to ensure that the existence of these Schedules is known to all their officers and to draw attention to the importance of the appointment of suitably qualified persons to act as "competent officers" for the purpose of discharging responsibility assumed under agreements with the Public Record Office.

'In our last Report we recommended that the Committee of Inspecting Officers of the Public Record Office and the representatives of Departments might, when appropriate, act in consultation with academic experts who could advise on the potential research value of particular records. We are pleased to note that effect is being given to this proposal....'[1]

The wording of this extract shows that, whatever improvement is now being made, the position in the past has not been at all satisfactory. Many of the returns rendered under the earlier Censuses of Production, and the associated files, are believed to have been destroyed, and it is hard to see what possible damage could have been done by preserving them for the use of economic historians in an approved library or research institute. Knowledge of the operations of an individual establishment in the year 1907 or 1912 could hardly be used to anyone's detriment in 1952 or after.

We are not satisfied that the arrangements for the prompt publication of non-confidential statistical material in departmental files are satisfactory. The North Committee, as we have seen (p. 14), is concerned with 'value for research purposes'; that is to say, primarily with obtaining facilities for individual research workers to have access to material, and not with its general publication. The advisory Committee proposed in the next chapter might well represent the public interest in prompt and adequate publication. Table 6 shows, for some representative statistical series, the interval before first publication.[2]

A glance at the table shows how valuable the device of a preliminary release can be. But the use of a press release may not be entirely satisfactory if newspapers for lack of space fail to publish the figures quickly or regularly. A possible solution is the incorporation in the existing weekly *Board of Trade Journal* of a statistical section in which the latest available statistics of all departments are published without delay. This course would avoid the necessity of developing an entirely new publication. Often, of course, an earlier release of a figure will mean that it is almost certain to be subject to subsequent revision, but this is also true to a lesser extent of the present practice. However, earlier first publication will make even more desirable the official adoption of the United States Department of Commerce practice of marking provisional figures with a '*p*' and the first publication of a subsequent revision with an '*r*'. This useful device enables users of the *Survey of Current Business* to keep track of alterations in important series without resorting to the laborious task of checking every single figure against the corresponding figure in the previous month's journal.

[1] [65b], p. 11.
[2] See also Table 7, p. 171. The American data are taken from Mills and Long [106], pp. 116–18.

Table 6. *Publication of representative statistical series*

Series	Frequency	First published		Approximate interval for nearest corresponding U.S. series, 1948
		In	After	
Employment	Monthly	Press release	4–5 weeks	9½ (preliminary in 4–5) weeks
Unemployment	Monthly	Press release	2–3 weeks	11 days (weekly)
Earnings	Half-yearly	*Ministry of Labour Gazette*	5–6 months	11½ (preliminary in 5½) weeks (monthly)
Wage rates	Monthly	*Ministry of Labour Gazette*	1 month	..
Industrial production index	Monthly	*Monthly Digest of Statistics* (press release 4 weeks*)	2 months (detail up to 5 months)	3–3½ weeks (revised 7 weeks)
Coal production	Weekly	Press release	3 days	1 week
Finished steel deliveries	Monthly	*British Iron and Steel Federation Bulletin*	2 months	..
Cotton yarn production	Monthly	*Board of Trade Journal*	6–7 weeks	..
Motor vehicle production	Monthly	*Monthly Digest of Statistics*	5–6 weeks	..
House completions	Monthly	*Housing Summary*	1 month	..
Numbers of live-stock	Quarterly	*Monthly Digest of Statistics*	3 months	6½ weeks (annual)
External trade: Value	Monthly	*Trade and Navigation Accounts* (press release 2 weeks*)	3 weeks	6–9 weeks
Volume index	Quarterly	*Board of Trade Journal*	6 weeks	2½ months (monthly)
Rail traffic receipts	Monthly	Press release	3–4 weeks	1 month
Bank deposits	Monthly	Press release	2–3 weeks	1 week (weekly)
Bank advances (detail)	Quarterly	Press release	3 weeks	..
Retail price indices	Monthly	Press release	4–5 weeks	5½ weeks
Wholesale price indices	Monthly	*Board of Trade Journal*	2 weeks	3½ weeks
Retail sales	Monthly	*Board of Trade Journal* (press release 4 weeks*)	5 weeks	3 weeks
Balance of payments	Half-yearly	White Paper	3½ months	..
Gold and dollar reserves	Monthly	Press release	2–3 days	..
National income estimates	Yearly	Blue Book	9 months (preliminary in 3 months)	3 months (quarterly)
Personal consumption	Quarterly	*Monthly Digest of Statistics*	2–3 months	..

* Only main figures usually appear in the press.

CONCLUSIONS

The official statisticians must present their compilations to people with, as has been seen, widely differing needs. There can be no possibility of operating three or four separate statistical services to cater for these varying requirements. The solution to the problem must inevitably be some kind of compromise.

Present practice is itself a compromise but rather a haphazard one. The Central Statistical Office only performs its function of centralized dissemination of information at rather a late stage; it exercises no detailed control over the preliminary release of statistics by individual departments. Nor can it at the moment ensure that adequate, accessible and up-to-date descriptions of all the series which are published are available. The improvement of the statistical service requires that users of statistics who require timely information should be able to subscribe to a centrally organized system of early releases over a much wider field of economic statistics, for example a modified *Board of Trade Journal* incorporating a special statistical section. This would mean that individual departments would have to devote more time to the compilation of provisional estimates. The Central Statistical Office in collaboration with the editors of the *Board of Trade Journal* should be responsible for collating and publishing all such early releases of information. In the United States, the *Survey of Current Business* issues a weekly four-page statistical summary giving about thirty weekly series of statistics and the first releases of nearly 200 other series.

The later revisions which would be made necessary would be published in the present *Monthly Digest of Statistics*. Such a scheme should apply both to basic statistics thrown up by the normal processes of administration and to derived statistics, such as the national income, balance of payments, and index of production. It would be most useful if more of the 'crude' data used in these derived statistics could be published, so that applied economists could provide their own private estimates. A determined effort needs to be made to keep up a speedy publication of the *Annual Abstract of Statistics*. This periodical would be more useful if it were supplemented by a new compilation, possibly published at three- or five-year intervals, giving a large number of series on a comparable basis for as long a run of years, or even months in some cases, as possible. Such a work would be a cross between the U.S. supplements to the *Survey of Current Business* and the publication called *Historical Statistics of the United States* [73].

In order that these extended services should be developed without involving an increased use of scarce statisticians, it would be necessary for very careful selection of the number and detail of series to be published to be undertaken. Rather than leave this selection to be determined by a knowledge of official requirements and surmises about what other people require, there would appear to be room for taking outside advice, in the manner proposed in the next chapter.

The official failure to provide enough information about the methods of compilation of various statistical series may possibly be ascribed to unwillingness to produce definitive versions of such descriptions while the methods themselves are in a continuing state of flux. This difficulty might well be overcome by the issue of descriptions which could be kept by the user in a loose-leaf folder. Such a device would enable all or part of the information about specific series to be cancelled or amended by the issue of a more up-to-date or comprehensive account. Where the current method of compilation was clearly likely to change rapidly, the description could be circulated in mimeographed form: while, where the technique seemed to be stable, printed descriptions could be issued. Once again it might be the function of the Central Statistical Office, urged on perhaps by an advisory committee, to supervise the circulation of these explanatory memoranda to all who cared to subscribe to the service.

These suggestions are not basically novel. Similar ones have been made with some force by F. C. Mills and C. D. Long in the United States.[1] Their detailed examination of American statistics revealed the same sort of faults that have been enumerated in this chapter, to wit, failure to publish or make accessible information of interest, delays in publication, and the lack of adequate published descriptions of statistical series.[2] Some American statisticians do, however, feel that too much is published in the United States and that the public interest would be better served by limiting the number of series so that attention is concentrated on the things that really matter.

The great improvement in the statistical services of the United Kingdom during the Second World War and after has been brought about in part by the vast extension of governmental activity throwing up a large statistical by-product and in part by the pressure within the civil service for more adequate information on which to base administrative decisions and advice to ministers. It is true that often such pressure was exercised by men who were not professional civil servants; for example, the late Lord Keynes encouraged and promoted the development of national income statistics. Nevertheless the influence of such men owed its success to the official positions from which it was exerted.

In this chapter the concern has been with the needs of users of statistics outside the civil service. At present there exists no adequate

[1] [106], pp. 136–9.　　　　[2] Ibid., pp. 114–20.

means by which they can encourage the statistical machine to adapt itself to their present and ever-changing requirements. We have tried to show where, in our opinion, changes are needed. The main recommendations made may be summarized as follows:

(1) The creation of a vehicle for the early production of facts, for example a modified *Board of Trade Journal*.

(2) The publication of signed articles by officials on matters of economic interest such as the balance of payments and the national income.

(3) The provision of more information about methods, sources of raw data, and possible errors.

(4) The publication at suitable intervals of an Abstract of Historical Statistics.

(5) The establishment of closer and more widespread contact between official providers and unofficial users of economic statistics.

CHAPTER XII

THE ORGANIZATION OF STATISTICAL INTELLIGENCE

The case-studies in the preceding chapters have shown something of the way in which statistical information is used as a basis for policy. But these individual studies do not tell us enough about the statistical system. What provision of economic statistics is required, not merely to provide for regular and foreseeable needs, but to meet unexpected demands? How should the collection and analysis of these statistics be organized?

THE NATURE OF A STATISTICAL SYSTEM

It may seem natural to think of the economic statistician as though he were an engineer, watching a set of dials attached to the economic machine and recording its temperature, its speed of working, its use or power and its output of product. But the analogy is misleading. The engineer's dials are part of the machine, planned to give information about variables which are known in advance to be important. The economic statistician's flow of information must be such as to give him warning of new problems which he may never have expected; and as these new problems command the interest of those in authority, he must be prepared to provide a stream of detailed information, showing how the difficulties have arisen and pointing the way to their solution. A better analogy is therefore with a military intelligence system, which has to provide a background of information against which decisions (of a varied and unpredictable nature) can be taken; but which must also stand ready, at short notice, to obtain detailed and frequent information about a particular sector of operations in which there are indications of unusual activity.

It must be noted that the statistician, though he can use intelligent foresight about the likely demands on his services, cannot even know all the current uses of his figures, let alone those which may arise in different circumstances in the future. He must be condemned if he spends his time collecting figures which, from their inherent nature, are *incapable* of further use; but it is not necessarily wrong for him to collect figures which are not currently being used, or whose current use is unknown to him. The difficulty is that, with limited resources, only part of the desirable background information can be provided. There will be pressure at each moment to employ those resources in providing information for the decisions of the moment; but the statistician has to preserve his flexibility, to keep unceasing watch on sectors of the front which are not at present active. This need to provide for the unknown future makes it especially difficult to decide the relative importance of different types of statistical investigation.

Even when a list of basic statistics for regular collection has been agreed, there will be the problem of organization to be tackled. On the one hand, many statistics are thrown up as a by-product of some administrative process, and it needs someone in close touch with administration to interpret the figures and understand their limitations. But if control of statistics is divided between a large number of administrative agencies, there may be overlapping, lack of co-ordination, and a wasteful use of competent statisticians. It is perhaps hardly likely that two agencies will set out to collect the same information—though even that is not unknown; but they may independently approach the same people on related matters, a form of overlapping which can be very irritating to the public. Furthermore, much trouble may be caused to the user of statistics by the use, by different agencies, of different schemes of classification—such as the varying lists of industries which were in use in Britain before the Standard Industrial Classification was prepared. It is still difficult to produce certain population statistics for the United Kingdom, because the three Registrars General have never agreed on a common form of presentation. The division of control may lead to a lowering of quality, because the smaller agencies will assign the preparation of statistics to people without proper training; or trained statisticians may find themselves loaded with administrative work, and unable to give proper attention to the practice of their science. The need for flexibility, of which we have spoken above, is more easily met by a central grouping of statisticians than by a scattering of them among different agencies.

These difficulties are general, and different countries have solved them in different ways. Before proceeding to examine in detail the problems as they present themselves in the United Kingdom, it will be helpful to look at the solutions tried in Canada and the United States. In Canada, statistical work is centralized in the Dominion Bureau of Statistics: in the United States, experiments in decentralization combined with co-ordination have been tried.

CANADA: AN EXPERIMENT IN CENTRALIZED CONTROL

As far back as 1887 Canada had a Chief Government Statistician, Dr George Johnson, who brought together a wide variety of statistical information into an annual *Statistical Abstract and Record of Canada*, the precursor of the present *Canada Year Book*. At that time, however, the actual collection of statistics was a departmental responsibility, and a special organization was created for the taking of each decennial census. In 1905 a permanent Census and Statistics Office was created, at first under the Department of Agriculture, and later under the Department of Trade and Commerce. This was initially a means of securing continuity of experience between censuses; but it naturally provided a nucleus for the co-ordination of general statistics. In 1912 a departmental commission was appointed to report on 'a comprehensive system of general statistics adequate to the necessities of the country and in keeping with the demands of the time'. Its report was an advanced document for its time, proposing (among other things) an annual census of production and a quinquennial census of population and property. But its key recommendation was the organization of a central statistical office, and in 1915 a Dominion Statistician was appointed and charged with the duty of preparing a scheme for such an office.

A memorandum, 'Statistical Organization in Canada' [76], prepared by the Dominion Bureau of Statistics in 1951, sets out the function of this office in a significant way. It was to 'control directly all statistics except those which are mere by-products of departmental administration, to supervise these latter so as to make them as useful as possible from the general point of view, and to establish a scheme of co-operation with Provincial Governments in order that statistics collected by the Provinces in the course of administration might be co-ordinated and compiled into Dominion totals'. The Dominion Bureau was created by the Statistics Act of 1918. It might be thought that most statistics are, at their original collection, mere by-products or adjuncts of administration; but this is clearly not the view held in Canada, and the Dominion Bureau itself collects and compiles the major statistical series. During the Second World War it was found necessary to set up separate statistical sections in war departments and agencies, to collect information needed (for instance) in the detailed administration of controls; but this reversion to partial departmental control was strictly temporary.

The Dominion Bureau's memorandum sets out several advantages of centralization, which 'has proved its worth in Canada.... There is widespread appreciation of the advantages of a co-ordinated overall statistical plan administered by one organization.' The advantages include: economical use of specialized talent, and of costly tabulating equipment; saving of time and energy in compiling 'overall' series, such as those of national income; saving of time for the public and for Government officials, who only have to go to one source for statistical data; public trust in the objectiveness of a central bureau; economic and effective liaison with the Provinces.

These advantages are considerable, especially in a small country. Thus the Republic of Ireland, which has a highly developed statistical system organized from a Central Statistics Office, would probably be quite unable to run efficient departmental statistical sections. But it is more significant that a centralized system works, with apparent success, in the much larger economy of Canada. As we shall see, there is a strongly held view in both the United States and Britain that it is dangerous to divorce statistics and administration, and that primary responsibility for the collection of statistics is usually best left with the different departments. It may be that what is still possible and desirable in Canada would be unworkable in a country with a more complex economy such as the United Kingdom; the fact that the Canadian statistical system had to be decentralized to some extent in order to link it to the complex administrative controls of wartime lends support to this view. On the other hand, it may be that the arguments in favour of departmental responsibility for statistics have been overworked. But it can be seen that the advantages claimed for a centralized system could for the most part be obtained by an effective *co-ordinating* agency—a central *collecting* agency is needed mainly to make effective use of skilled personnel and specialized equipment. This need is certainly less pressing in a larger country. The United States provides an example of decentralized collection and central co-ordination which we will now discuss.

THE UNITED STATES EXPERIENCE

The experience of the United States in statistical organization has been recorded in a convenient way by Linnenberg.[1] In 1908 Theodore Roosevelt set up an Interdepartmental Statistical Committee, drawn from ten agencies, for purposes of co-ordination and improvement; but this Committee was apparently short-lived. In 1918–19 the exceptional needs of war brought into being a Central Bureau of Planning and Statistics. In 1922 the Bureau of Efficiency proposed a permanent office, a Bureau of Federal Statistics, within which the 'collection, tabulation and dissemination of all non-administrative statistics' would have been 'centralized, so far as practicable'. It should be noted that 'non-administrative' appears to mean 'not developed for purposes of detailed administration'; so that most of the statistics required as a basis for economic policy, which are the subject of this report, would presumably have been prepared or at least processed in the Bureau proposed.

However, no action was taken, and the next major step had to wait until April 1931. By Budget Circular 293 there was established a

[1] [104].

Federal Statistics Board of sixteen members drawn from various departments. Linnenberg quotes:

'It shall be the duty of the Federal Statistics Board to study the existing situation with regard to the collection, compilation, dissemination and utilization of statistics by agencies of the Federal Government and to make recommendations to the Chief Coordinator looking to the elimination of needless duplication in statistical work and the fullest possible utilization of statistical information collected and the personnel and facilities concerned therewith, as well as the most effective and economical means of procuring additional statistics for which there may be a reasonable demand.'

But the Board, having neither staff nor powers, was largely ineffective. By Executive Order under the National Industrial Recovery Act, President Roosevelt established in its place a Central Statistical Board (July 1933). This Board had a small secretariat, and it was given power 'to advise upon all schedules of all Government agencies engaged in the primary collection of statistics required in carrying out the purposes of the National Industrial Recovery Act, to review plans for tabulation and classification of such statistics, and to promote coordination and improvement of the statistical services involved'. We see here the beginnings of one of the main ideas of U.S. statistical organization; that a central agency should advise on the preparation of forms and schedules. This may have a direct effect in improving their statistical quality; but it also gives the central agency a record of the statistical work of the departments, timely warning of new activities, and a means of preventing overlapping.

In May 1934 a further Executive Order broadened the interests of the Board to cover Federal and non-Federal statistical services in the United States useful to the recovery programme. It was authorized to undertake experimental statistical activities and (subject to the consent of the agency concerned) to investigate any statistical service within its scope, and to publish its conclusions. In July 1935 another reorganization took place; by Public Law 219 Congress gave the Board a statutory mandate. The Board was now to have a paid chairman, appointed by the President and confirmed by the Senate, and thirteen other members at most, of whom at least ten were to be already in the service of the United States. It was now given a general power of investigation of existing or proposed statistical work of Federal agencies; the power to investigate non-Federal work, subject to consent, remained. A staff, and appropriations not exceeding $180,000 per year, were authorized.

In November 1936, Regulation 1 under Law 219 required every Federal agency to submit for review prior to adoption all 'general questionnaires' (that is forms for asking, or recording answers to, questions and sent to twenty or more respondents). This gave the Board and its staff an opportunity of offering advice, but there was no power to require that the advice should be taken. In July 1939 the Bureau of the Budget was made part of the Executive Office of the President, instead of being in the Treasury, and the Central Statistical Board was placed under the control of the Bureau's Director. The staff of the Board became known as the Division[1] of Statistical Standards in the Bureau of the Budget. Budget Circular 360 of June 1940 superseded Regulation 1 of the Central Statistical Board, giving the Division broadly the same powers as before—requiring *automatic* submission of all new report forms, while plans for tabulation, analysis or publication were to be submitted on request. But the Division could still only offer advice. Its governing body, the Central Statistical Board, ceased to exist in July 1940, when Law 219 expired; thereafter, the work of the Division was undertaken under the Bureau's general powers derived from the Budget and Accounting Act of 1921, and the Executive order setting out the functions of the Bureau.

In 1942 the screw of co-ordination was tightened a little further. A supplement to Circular 360, issued in August of that year, required that after 1 January 1943 'every report form used by any (Federal) agency shall bear an approval number assigned to it by the Bureau of the Budget'. The Division of Statistical Standards was thus given power to require that its advice should be taken; and it also became necessary to review all forms already in use.

This action was quickly followed by the passing of the Federal Reports Act of 1942, which gave the Bureau of the Budget very wide powers over nearly all information-gathering activities of Federal agencies. This Act requires that agencies (with a few specified exceptions) shall obtain Budget Bureau approval in advance for every questionnaire or other request for information to be sent to ten or more respondents. Furthermore, it gives the Director of the Bureau instructions to investigate, at intervals, the needs of Federal agencies for information and their methods used in obtaining it. He is to co-ordinate information collecting services, and may after due inquiry and hearing designate a single 'collecting agency' to obtain information for two or more agencies. If he finds that an agency is collecting information which it could obtain elsewhere or which is not needed, he can require the collection to stop. He can require (subject to specified safeguards of confidentiality) that one agency should disgorge information to another.

The wider powers given in this way were given 'teeth' by Regulation A in 1943 (revised as Budget Circular No. A-40 in 1948), which replaced Circular 360. This regulation describes the procedures to be followed

[1] Re-named 'Office' (1952).

by agencies in requesting clearance and the considerations to be taken into account by the Bureau in its review—such as, for example, number of respondents, frequency of collection, and number and difficulty of the items asked. It also describes standard notations for the Budget Bureau approval number to appear on each form, as evidence that it has been reviewed and approved.

The purposes of the Budget Bureau examination are to prevent unnecessary duplication, reduce costs, minimize reporting burdens, and improve the quality and general usefulness of the statistics obtained. The number of review 'actions' was as high as 8,000 a year during the Second World War, and is now about 3,500 a year. The disapproval rate, which was 12 % in the first year of operations under the Federal Reports Act, has steadily declined as a result of more general understanding and acceptance of the criteria to be met and increasingly careful review within the agencies before formal requests for clearance from the Budget Bureau.

In 1945, the Director of the Bureau reported to the House Committee on Appropriations on the state of co-ordination reached (Congressional Record, vol. 91, part 13, pp. A5419–5423). His arguments may be summarized as follows:

(1) Repeated investigations had confirmed that complete centralization of fact-gathering is impossible, but that central co-ordination is necessary.

(2) Centralization is impossible because:

(a) Many statistics arise in the course of administration, and it is more efficient to deal with them through the staff in charge of administration. Separation would tend to increase costs.

(b) Specialist knowledge of particular fields is required in obtaining, analysing and interpreting statistics: it would be wasteful to have to provide specialists in both an administrative agency and a central statistical office.

(c) Accuracy and timeliness would be reduced in a mammoth central agency.

(3) The Budget Bureau achieves co-ordination:

(a) through its review of forms,

(b) by establishing single collecting agencies,

(c) by developing uniform standards (for example of industrial or commodity classification),

(d) through its knowledge of the work of agencies, achieved especially because of its annual review of appropriation requests.

One further step to strengthen this co-ordinating system was taken in the Budget and Accounting Procedures Act of 1950, which followed on the report of the Hoover Commission on Organization of the Executive

Branch of the Government. The Hoover Commission had before it a comprehensive evaluation of Federal statistical services made by Frederick C. Mills and Clarence D. Long of the National Bureau of Economic Research. The Mills-Long report recommended a degree of centralization in collection; it proposed that the Bureau of the Census should undertake the primary collection of statistics gathered on a repetitive basis and for which highly specialized knowledge of subject-matter is not required in the collection process. It also proposed that the field offices of the Census Bureau should be used by other agencies to collect statistics. It is clear that, under this plan, only 'highly specialized' statistics would be left for regular collection by separate departments. In practice, most really large-scale field inquiries in the United States are already undertaken by the Census Bureau. It is worth noting that a powerful impetus has been given towards the central *processing* of statistics by the development of electronic machines, whose expense would seldom be justified for a single department. The Canadian Census of 1951 is being processed on such a machine.

The Hoover Commission did not go as far as Mills and Long, but it recommended that the co-ordinating authority of the Division of Statistical Standards should be strengthened. This recommendation is carried out by S. 103 of the Budget and Accounting Procedures Act (see Stuart Rice, *American Statistician*, 1950, vol. 4, no. 5):

'The President, through the Director of the Bureau of the Budget, is authorized and directed to develop programs, and to issue regulations and orders for the improved gathering, compiling, analysing, publishing and dissemination of statistical information for any purpose by the various agencies in the executive branch of the Government. Such regulations and orders shall be adhered to by such agencies.'

This section applies only to *statistical* information, whereas the Federal Reports Act covers all information-gathering activities; but it will be noted that whereas the earlier Act emphasizes collection, this Act gives equal emphasis to 'compiling, analysing, publishing and dissemination'. With the 1950 Act, the United States appears to have gone about as far as is possible in strengthening central control while maintaining departmental responsibility for collecting statistics.[1]

---

[1] See also Rice [113], Copeland [94], Tukey [117], and Hansen and Long [98].

PRESENT ORGANIZATION IN THE UNITED KINGDOM

The United States experience is one of the steady growth of precise co-ordinating powers. In contrast, the United Kingdom system is informal, based on custom and habit rather than on the assignment of exact responsibilities.

The shortcomings of the pre-war statistical system in Britain are forcibly outlined in the Royal Statistical Society's 1943 *Memorandum on Official Statistics*.[1] The responsibility for collecting statistics was divided between many departments, some without a separate statistical branch; figures were collected in the wrong form, their analysis and use was inadequate, and there was little opportunity for a department to acquire a fully trained statistical staff. Co-ordination was nominally the function of a Permanent Consultative Committee on Official Statistics, appointed as a result of a petition of the Society in 1919. 'It comprised representatives of the major Departments under the chairmanship of Sir Alfred Watson, the Government Actuary, and later of Sir Frederick Leith-Ross. It was unwieldy, and had no initiatory powers, being able only to consider matters referred to it by Departments. We think it fair to say that the Committee exercised little influence on departmental practice and that by the outbreak of war it was moribund.'[2] The Board of Trade was responsible for the *Statistical Abstract*, and was in a sense the major statistical department; and there was, of course, a good deal of informal contact, outside the Permanent Committee, between the official statisticians.

All this, however, fell much short of an adequate degree of co-ordination. No one who has had prolonged experience of working with the statistics of the 1930's can fail to have noticed the extreme difficulty of using them together to depict the economic structure. Systems of classification differed; apparent contradictions were difficult to resolve without laborious research. Furthermore, there were large gaps in our knowledge of most of the principal economic variables. Production statistics were patchy, and data on expenditure were almost non-existent. Most important of all, the integration of estimates into a single record of economic change and of the interrelationship of the parts of the economy had only been attempted by private individuals.

Early in the Second World War, the importance of economic policy to the development of a maximum war effort was recognized by the establishment of two Economic Policy Committees, one at official and one at Ministerial level. The Chairman of the official committee, Lord Stamp, was himself a distinguished worker in the fields of national income and capital. Together with Sir Henry Clay and Sir Hubert

[1] [116].   [2] Ibid.

Henderson, he had been called in the summer of 1939 to assist the Treasury in the assessment of economic plans; and as the problems of economic policy became apparent, a further group of economists was called in and (at the end of 1939) a Central Economic Information Service was started. When Mr Churchill's Government took office, in May 1940, a system of Cabinet Committees was created—one each for Production, Economic Policy, Food Policy and Home Policy; and these were co-ordinated by a committee under the chairmanship of the Lord President of the Council. At this stage the Central Economic Information Service was in effect the staff of the Minister without Portfolio, Mr Greenwood, as Chairman of the Economic Policy Committee. In January 1941 the duties of the Economic Policy Committee, in relation to general economic policy, were transferred to the Lord President's Committee; just before this happened, the Information Service was split into two parts. One became the Economic Section of the War Cabinet Offices; under Professor Jewkes, and later Professor Robbins, Professor Meade, and Mr R. L. Hall, it acted as an economic staff to the Lord President of the Council (Sir John Anderson, now Lord Waverley). This section continues as part of the Cabinet Offices, and is responsible for keeping the Cabinet supplied with material for its review and planning of economic policy.

The second product of this fission, led by Mr Francis Hemming (shortly afterwards, and to the present day, by Mr H. Campion, C.B.) became the Central Statistical Office. There was also during Mr Churchill's premiership a small group called the Prime Minister's Statistical Section; this ceased to exist in 1945, but was revived when Mr Churchill again became Premier in 1951. The purpose of this Section was to prepare material—statistics, charts, and diagrams—for the personal use of the Prime Minister; but it also acted in effect as a group of private advisers, ranging over the whole field of war production and economic policy, and it thus aided the Prime Minister's co-ordination of policy by giving him a source of ideas independent of his departmental Ministers.

The purpose of both the Economic Section and the Prime Minister's Section was, and is, to give advice—one to the Cabinet in general through its Minister responsible for economic co-ordination, the other to the Prime Minister personally through his personal Adviser, Lord Cherwell. There is also an Information Division in the Treasury whose main function is the preparation of material for the public (for example press releases). The Central Statistical Office was set apart from these; on the one hand it has no advisory functions on policy, and therefore could be claimed to be free from the bias which might come from being an advocate of a particular policy; on the other hand, it has no propaganda functions, and its publications are related solely to statistical facts and techniques.

The interrelations of these bodies are made more difficult to understand because of the varying subtleties of their relations to the Treasury. The Prime Minister holds office by virtue of being First Lord of the Treasury; the Treasury vote bears his salary and that of his personal staff, and also the salary of the Secretary to the Cabinet and his staff. The Economic Section and the Central Statistical Office were both sub-sections of the Offices of the Cabinet, which is technically a 'subordinate department' of the Treasury. In practice they have been almost independent of the Treasury; on economic matters there was[1] often an 'Economic Section view' as well as a 'Treasury view'. But the degree of independence depends on whether there is, as in wartime, a Minister without departmental responsibilities who co-ordinates economic policy. To a strong Chancellor of the Exchequer, such as Sir Stafford Cripps, the Economic Section and the Treasury became in effect joint advisers. Since their relation is liable to fluctuate with changes in the Cabinet, it was perhaps convenient to separate the technical work of the Statistical Office from the channels of advice. But in the centre, as in the departments, there is a danger in drawing a line between objective fact-finding and the preparation of policy. The fact-finders may not really be more objective, and they will tend to be less well informed about what is really needed. They may waste their energy in turning out figures which no one uses. The statistician in the Central Statistical Office is a kind of wholesaler of statistics, and he gets his knowledge both of the manufacturing process which turns out the figures, and of the public and official demand which 'consumes' them, at second hand. This is a difficult situation to be in, and it is not therefore obvious that the precise separation of functions now achieved is the best possible.[2]

The nature of the functions of the Central Statistical Office have recently been described.[3] From the standpoint of this study, the most important activity of the C.S.O. has been to bring together statistical data from various departments into the comprehensive economic record of the National Income publications. This has involved the preparation of many new estimates; some of these have been made 'in the departments', some in the C.S.O., but the C.S.O. has had the important function of fitting them into a common logical framework, and of adjusting the estimates to secure consistency. Apart from this vital group of statistics, the C.S.O. does not itself prepare material except where interdepartmental co-ordination is required (for example the

---

[1] The Economic Section has now been absorbed into the main structure of the Treasury.
[2] The wartime history is set out in 'Lessons of the British War Economy' [93], and this is the source of much of the above summary.   [3] [60].

Index of Industrial Production); and in no case is it an original collecting agency, requests to the public for information being made through other departments.

In another sense, however, the C.S.O. has important 'collecting' functions; namely, in bringing together statistics from departmental records and in presenting them, first to Ministers and departments, and then to the public. The *Monthly Digest* and *Annual Abstract of Statistics* have, under the C.S.O., set new standards of statistical presentation, not only for Britain but for the world. A beginning has also been made on the task of giving adequate technical background to the statistics—through the notes annually published on the statistics in the *Monthly Digest*, and through the series of monographs 'Studies in Official Statistics'. Behind the scenes, the C.S.O. acts for other departments as a technical advisory body to which one would naturally turn for information not obviously obtainable elsewhere, and which can be expected to help in reconciling estimates from different sources or in assessing their accuracy.

There is no doubt that, in the course of its work, the C.S.O. has greatly improved the co-ordination and presentation of British statistics. Its members tend to have wide contacts with departmental statisticians, both informally and in Committee work. There is an increasing tendency for the principal departmental statistical posts to be filled by men with C.S.O. experience. But the formal powers of the Office are similar to those of the United States Central Statistical Board about 1935; it has no means of coercing a department to adopt a particular statistical technique, and there is nothing corresponding to the compulsory clearance of forms through the Division of Statistical Standards or to the wide powers of direction of statistical programmes given in the United States by S. 103 of the 1950 Budget Act.

Although there is no collecting agency in the United Kingdom with the wide interests of the United States Bureau of the Census, there is a field-work agency, the Social Survey, which undertakes sampling inquiries for other Departments through its field staff. Some aspects of its work have been described in a paper by Gray and Corlett,[1] and an appendix to the paper lists some of the inquiries carried out in the years 1946 to 1949. According to our information, these are also representative of more recent work: the following examples show that the inquiries include some concerned with fact and some with opinion:

Survey of the incidence of illness and injury	*for* the Registrar General (England and Wales)
Study of the impact of the Road Safety Publicity Campaign	*for* the Ministry of Transport

[1] [96].

Survey of attitudes to employment in the civil service	*for* the Treasury
Estimate of future demand for carpets	*for* the Board of Trade
Study of the incidence of deafness and the demand for hearing aids	*for* the Medical Research Council
Inquiry into the leisure activities of children	*for* the Ministry of Education
Inquiry into lighting in offices	*for* the Department of Scientific and Industrial Research
Inquiries into the nutrition of housewives	*for* the Ministry of Health
Inquiries into certain types of consumer expenditure	*for* the Central Statistical Office

The last example is an important one—it shows how a special sampling agency is beginning to be used to derive basic statistics for the social accounts. There is room for development of this specialization.

IS THE BRITISH ORGANIZATION ADEQUATE?

We think that it will readily be agreed that a degree of statistical centralization such as that in Canada would be very difficult to impose on the larger and more complex economy of the United Kingdom, and would involve an undesirable separation of the statistician and the administrator. It is tempting to suppose that the difference between the precise co-ordinating powers adopted in the United States and the loose and informal relationships developed in the United Kingdom is no more than a difference of national habit; that, with its supposed genius for 'muddling through' and for making the illogical work, Britain can achieve by informality as much as anyone else can achieve by regulation.

It is true that the difference between the United States and Britain is less than appears on the surface. The necessary condition of success in any co-ordination is friendly relations between the parties; and it is clear that the American system will only work in so far as the Office of Statistical Standards maintains friendly and informal relations with the agencies over whose statistical activities it has ultimate powers of direction. But, after considering the results of our investigation, we cannot give quite full marks to the British system. We suggest that eight questions have to be answered:

(i) Does it make a satisfactory impact on policy?

(ii) Is the system *comprehensive*, that is, does it give that 'intelligence background' mentioned on p. 140 above?

(iii) Is it *flexible*? Can detailed information on particular matters be obtained quickly?

(iv) Is it *well integrated*? Are inconsistencies speedily observed and removed?

(v) Does it make a satisfactory *impact on the public*? Are duplication, the keeping of unnecessary records and the filling up of bad or unnecessary forms eliminated?

(vi) Does it give uniform and high *standards of statistical technique*?

(vii) Is it efficient in its use of statistical *manpower*?

(viii) Is it *efficient* in *money cost*?

THE IMPACT ON POLICY

One of the original reasons for establishing the Central Statistical Office was to prevent inconsistent estimates from being used in interdepartmental discussions, or by different Ministers in the Cabinet. The facts were to be ascertained, as nearly as possible, and were then to be used as agreed data. The statistical system is certainly much nearer than it was in 1939 to this ideal of talking with one voice. But it does not follow that the voice is being listened to by the policy-makers, or that it is saying things relevant to their needs. As we have explained before (Chapter 1), it is impossible for the outsider to follow in detail the use of statistics in the preparation of policy. It is probably difficult for the official statistician to follow the uses made of some of his figures. The (otherwise welcome) improvement in the status of statisticians in the Government tends to make them 'experts' with few administrative functions and no direct responsibility for policy. We think it most important that the heads of statistics divisions, at least, should be as far as possible directly involved in the preparation of policy—not just as experts, called in to give special advice. To some extent this already happens; it seems to us desirable that it should happen more, though this must not imply that the official statisticians should become any less expert in their own subject.

COMPREHENSIVENESS

This is not the place to list the gaps in British economic statistics. They are not at the moment numerous, though they include some important items, such as the serious lack of knowledge of trade stocks. The question to be considered is whether the present organization of British statistics is such as to promote comprehensiveness. On the whole there is (since the development of social accounting) no serious ground for complaint. The social accounts require in their preparation a wide range of statistics, and several important gaps (for example consumer expenditure) have been filled since 1939 as a consequence of the preparation of these accounts. The demands of the C.S.O. have stimulated the departments to provide the necessary information, and this process is likely to continue; and, considering the excellent progress made since 1940, there seems no reason to think that progress would have been more rapid under a different form of organization. There are, however, areas of statistical information which need not be surveyed for the present system of national accounts, and which may tend to be neglected; regional statistics[1] are an example. It is important that the staff of the C.S.O. should be large enough to keep a watch on such material.

FLEXIBILITY

The needs of policy-makers for information will vary from month to month; and at times there will be exceptional demands for information about a particular piece or aspect of the economic system—for example a particular industry thought suitable for public ownership. Such demands can sometimes be met from the general body of background information—for example from a Census of Production—and sometimes from a special analysis of existing data—for example a special tabulation from the Trade Accounts. But it may be necessary to gather new data in the field, and it will certainly be necessary to find trained people to do the required research. A small department is not easily able to meet such special calls; indeed, greater flexibility would be one of the advantages of complete centralization of Government statistics. In a small country, unable to employ specialist statisticians in its separate departments, the need for flexibility may itself be a convincing reason for centralization. In Britain, where the major departments (such as the Board of Trade) have substantial Statistics Divisions, the argument is less convincing. In practice, the factor limiting flexibility has not been any failure of organization, but the acute shortage of statistical manpower; and we have tried to propose, in our later discussion of this matter, ways of increasing the use of common services which might in themselves increase flexibility.

[1] For one region, the semi-autonomous State of Northern Ireland, important statistical information is lacking and other information is available only on a basis different from that used in Great Britain. In consequence some United Kingdom statistics are in fact estimates based on data for Great Britain only. It would seem proper for the Imperial Government to represent to the Northern Ireland Government that there is no advantage to either party in this lack of co-ordination.

INTEGRATION

The need to reconcile different estimates, in order to bring them within the framework of the social accounts, has had a beneficial effect on the degree of integration of British statistics. The C.S.O., behind the scenes, has encouraged the elimination of unnecessary differences, and such pieces of interdepartmental co-operation as the adoption of the Standard Industrial Classification, and the more general use of Standard Regions, have greatly improved the possibilities of comparison between different types of economic statistics.

But there is another aspect of integration—one which might equally well be considered in our later discussion of efficiency. Different types of statistics are often collected from the same 'universe'; for example, the universe of industrial establishments, or of shops, or of companies. It seems to us doubtful if enough thought has been given to the maintenance of a register of the universe by the most efficient methods, and to the use of a common list with the same classification by all departments obtaining information from those on the register.

An example is to be found in the first Census of Distribution, taken in respect of the trading year 1950. The mailing list for this census was specially prepared by an elaborate method, involving personal interviews as well as searches of directories. It is to be hoped that the Census will provide a basis for designing new samples for the retail trade statistics, and that it will itself be repeated at intervals. We believe, however, that no provision has been made for the maintenance of an up-to-date register. But it seems to us that the register required is essentially a sub-section of a complete list of business premises by their geographical locations, and that such a list could be compiled and kept up to date in each locality as a by-product of the valuations for Schedule A and for local rates. At present (we are told) the rating lists are useless for this purpose, since it is impossible to tell whether such an entry as 'house with garage' refers to a private house with a garage or to the establishment of a motor repairer. This is a fault easily corrected; and it seems to us that a comprehensive list of all premises at which it is believed that a business or trade is carried on would be valuable, both as a basis for constructing other registers, and as a means of checking lists obtained by other means (for example from factory inspectors). The cost to the Inland Revenue Department of maintaining such a list could hardly exceed the cost of constructing a special Census list of all shops every five years or so.

We understand that in the industrial field there has been some confusion, owing to different departments classifying the same establishment in different ways. There is, of course, often difficulty in deciding on the industrial classification of a factory which makes several products; and a classification by 'establishments' will differ from one by 'firms' (for example, Census of Production and Inland Revenue data are difficult to reconcile). But all bodies requiring an industrial classification by establishments should, one would suppose, have access to a common list of establishments with code numbers indicating their classification. This appears to exist at the centre, but not to be effective in the local offices where statistics often start their life. We believe, however, that it is possible for a worker to be classified to one industry by the Ministry of National Insurance or the Ministry of Labour, and to another in the labour returns of the Census of Production. No doubt such differences are removed in time, but they should not be allowed to arise.

It would be a great convenience if the lists of companies, compiled as a result of the registration requirements, were to bear code numbers indicating an industrial classification corresponding to that used for Inland Revenue purposes. No confidential information would be revealed by such a coding, and it would make possible a much-needed reclassification of financial statistics on a common basis. The *Stock Exchange List*, the *Financial Times* lists of share prices, *The Economist's* statistics of company profits and balance sheets, the data on bank advances by trades, and the Inland Revenue statistics need to be brought, as nearly as possible, to the same classification.

These instances suggest that the C.S.O. at present may be ineffective (perhaps because its members are too busy) in pressing reforms which involve changes of administrative practice in addition to agreement between statisticians. There is something to be said for the generality of the United States Federal Reports Act in dealing with all 'information'. The material which flows into Government files may be needed for different purposes, some statistical, some administrative, and the attainment of true integration needs to be sought at a higher level than that of the technical statistician. A broad and imaginative view of the requirements of Government in its relations with citizens and businesses is needed, so that the information is gathered and processed ready for different uses, and so that it will be classified by different users in the same way. Great progress has been made, but there is more to be done.

THE IMPACT ON THE PUBLIC

The last section suggests that there may be room for economy in approach to the public—for example by forming registers which can be used for different purposes. But it is worth while studying the impact of statistical investigation on the public in a wider sense. The unwillingness of the 'man in the street', and even of the business man, to answer questions is often exaggerated; but this does not mean that the quality of the approach made to the public can be neglected. The ordinary citizen needs to feel that the information for which he is asked is necessary, that it is being collected in a way which has regard to his convenience, and that the questions which he has to answer are such that he may reasonably be expected to know the answer. A good deal of prejudice against 'bureaucrats' arises from a feeling that the bureaucrat has regard only to his own convenience; and much inaccuracy in statistical returns can come from their asking questions which cannot reasonably be answered from the records of the respondent. A possible example from the building industry was given in a preceding chapter (p. 119).

To some extent the interest of the general public is provided for in the United Kingdom by Advisory Committees, such as the Census of Production Committees, which help to decide what questions should be asked in each census. But we think that there might be some advantage in a modified version of the United States centralized review of forms, which would ensure that there was a group of people whose primary interest was to secure a reasonable and convenient approach to the public. A number of the forms we have seen (including one requiring unusual tact, the Income Tax return) appear to us capable of minor improvement; and some overlapping, or unreasonable, requests for information might be eliminated in the course of the review.

STATISTICAL STANDARDS

As we have seen, the use of sampling has not been carried very far in British economic statistics; if it is more generally adopted, more people with mathematical qualifications and with a knowledge of sampling techniques will be required. At present there is little use of anything but the most elementary statistical methods in the day-to-day work of the Government economic statisticians. Their activity may, however, extend in directions which would require the use of more refined techniques; a good deal of work on demand analysis is, for instance, needed.

We cannot help feeling, also, that a more imaginative approach to statistics would result in more use of techniques designed to give *relevant* answers *quickly*—as, for instance, by specially designed sample inquiries. We think, therefore, that in future more central help to departments on matters of statistical technique will be needed. We do not suggest any imposed uniformity—some variety of practice is useful; the present informal help given by the C.S.O. could, given sufficient staff, be extended.

158 BRITISH ECONOMIC STATISTICS

EFFICIENCY

It will be convenient to discuss the last two criteria, efficiency in the use of men and of money, together. The need for economy in Government expenditure, and for making the best use of funds allocated, is obvious. But competent statisticians are even harder to get than money. The output of men and women who have taken courses in statistics is now considerable, but many of these lack the breadth of understanding which is needed in the economic field. Like the master-economist in Keynes's celebrated description,[1] the economic statistician '...must understand symbols and speak in words. He must contemplate the particular in terms of the general, and touch abstract and concrete in the same flight of thought. He must study the present in the light of the past for the purposes of the future.' There are few who understand both their material and their method, who can have an imaginative sense of the layman's difficulty both in providing and in interpreting statistical data; and of these few, industry now attracts a good proportion by paying high salaries. It is usual, therefore, for there to be unfilled posts in the establishment of the C.S.O. and the departmental statistical divisions.

We must, however, keep a sense of proportion in this matter. Mills and Long record that, in the year ended 30 June 1948, United States Federal agencies employed 10,385 people on statistical work (outside military departments), and that the cost of statistical services was $42 million. These are less than 1 % of Federal civilian employment and non-military expenditure.[2] Comparable figures for the United Kingdom are not available, but it is clear that the total size of the statistical divisions is much less than in the United States—small even in relation to our smaller population and area. In any case, the total employment consists largely of clerical workers; a more significant figure is the number in the Statistician Class—that is, the skilled men and women who direct the work.

This number is some 50 or 60; and it is indeed remarkable that so comprehensive a statistical system depends on the devoted labours of so few. In the long run it should surely be possible to devise means of training which will expand their number, and to demonstrate that some extra funds granted for statistical work would save a greater value in waste elsewhere.

In the short run, however, the shortage of men and money is a very serious limitation, and it means that we have to be cautious in recommending extensions of statistical work. If there is to be an adequate system of statistical intelligence it will need to be planned as a whole, and some authority will have to judge the relative importance of

[1] [103].   [2] [106], p. 4.

different types of statistics and match extensions in one field against economies in another. As we have suggested above, 'importance' is not to be identified with 'degree of present use'; it is a matter of judgement, requiring an imaginative assessment of possible future uses in different circumstances.

One only has to state the needs in this form to see the great difficulty of meeting them in a decentralized system. If (as seems to us possible) labour statistics have attained an elaboration which is not fully utilized,[1] while inventory statistics are rudimentary, it would seem sensible to restore the balance by transferring resources from one field to the other. But this would be a transfer between different Ministries; the Ministry of Labour will not wish to abridge activities which are in themselves desirable enough, and if it is forced to do so as an economy it will not be easy to arrange that expenditure should expand correspondingly in the Ministry of Supply or the Board of Trade.

Nevertheless the need for making the best possible allocation of scarce statistical resources is a serious one. We suggest that it would be useful to form, under the wing of the C.S.O., a Committee to bring Government economic statistics under regular review.[2] This Committee should include, in addition to representative official statisticians, senior administrators and (if possible) 'outside' economists and statisticians; its membership should be such as to carry considerable weight within the civil service. The recommendations of such a Committee could strengthen the hands of a departmental Statistical Division, in asking for an increase in its staff and budget; while the absence of approval could serve as a hint to those responsible for preparing or examining Estimates that economies could be made in the statistical services of the department concerned. It is not reasonable to expect the C.S.O. itself to undertake this reviewing function, since it is a competitor for the resources to be allocated; and the decision as to whether available first-rate statisticians should be spread among the departments, or concentrated in the C.S.O., is one of the major items for the Committee's agenda.

In making this recommendation we are not forgetting the United States experience that Committee 'advice' without powers of control is ineffective. We think, however, that the tradition of co-operation, strengthened by the wise policy of the C.S.O., is sufficient to make an Advisory Committee in this country effective. But, in order that this may be so, we think it important that its membership should be such as to carry weight.

The efficient production of statistics demands more than a reallocation of resources between the present producers. The methods of

[1] Another example of unnecessary elaboration is the weekly figure of coal consumption.
[2] It could review also (as suggested in Chapter XI) matters of availability and publication.

production also need review, and so does the fitness of the final product for its users. We should welcome more 'efficiency studies' of British statistics, which would examine in fuller detail the kind of material which we have discussed in the earlier chapters of this book. To take one example, is speed of publication important enough to the users to outweigh a danger of greater error? Many users of the Census of Production have come to feel that the results of a full census take so long to analyse that they have lost much of their usefulness by the time that they appear; and that it would therefore be, in a proper sense, more 'efficient' to devise a sample census whose results, though subject to sampling error, would be more timely. We are glad to note that this is now being done.

It is, indeed, arguable that too much energy is spent in many fields on obtaining complete returns, and that sample surveys might be not only more rapid but more accurate—their sampling error being offset by the greater ease of ensuring full and correct response. American colleagues have represented to us that the reliance upon complete censuses in this country means also a reliance on postal questionnaires, and that a sampling system would bring the cost of personal visits (generally a more effective way of obtaining correct information) to a reasonable figure. There seem to us to be two matters here which need investigation. First, a change-over from complete to sample surveys would save mainly in clerical staff, and in trouble to the respondents; but it might mean the use of *more* trained statisticians, since there would be more technical problems to be dealt with. Secondly, a fuller use of personal investigation would seldom be justified for the purposes of a single inquiry; for it would be difficult to recruit and train a staff spread all over the country. Is it worth while considering whether, perhaps as a development of the Social Survey, there should be established a 'field investigation' staff for the joint use of several agencies?

These are questions which cannot be answered without drawing up costings, in money and manpower, for the alternative methods. *Prima facie*, there is a strong case for a fuller use of sampling—for example, for most Censuses of Production and Distribution, for obtaining population data, for some monthly production and consumption statistics, and for labour statistics. There is quite a good case, on grounds not only of efficiency but of flexibility, for establishing a field organization for sampling, capable of collecting several types of statistics. We welcome the progress which has been made in the use of sampling, but should like to see our proposed Advisory Committee investigate the matter further.

CONCLUSION

The conclusion to which these sections have led is certainly not one which condemns the present organization of British statistics. It is friendly and informal, and on the whole it has worked well in the last twelve years. It is also a little haphazard, and we are not sure that it is so arranged that enough attention can be given to general issues such as we discuss in this book. The pressure of day-to-day work is usually overwhelming. We have proposed, therefore, various marginal changes which would increase the influence of the C.S.O. and ensure that the planning of statistical intelligence should be conscious and not haphazard. We have not suggested the adoption of precise powers of control, such as those of the United States Office of Statistical Standards; we think that something more informal, half-way between the American and the present British system, would be appropriate to our needs.

CHAPTER XIII

POSTSCRIPT

A great many ideas and suggestions—some, we think, important, and some perhaps trivial—appear in the course of the preceding report. To save the reader trouble in tracing them, we have allotted a separate section of the Index to a table of proposals. But it would give a false impression if, like a Royal Commission, we were now to set down a carefully rounded set of definite recommendations. One of the reasons why we ask that there should be a central Advisory Committee on statistics is so that some of the subjects we have discussed may be looked at *with* the official statisticians, and with the benefit of all their knowledge of what is wanted and of what is possible, which we from outside cannot hope to equal.

The central message of this report, then, is the need for new and fundamental thinking about the British statistical system. We are proud of that system, and of the standards which it has set; we notice that in fields such as social accounting British statisticians have been leaders in the development of basic theory as well as in practical applications. We recognize the tremendous improvements which have taken place in the last fourteen years. But we should like to see British statistics continue to be progressive and pioneering, and we are not sure if this will be so unless there is a chance of fresh thought.

We should like to see, for instance, statistics made available to their users in imaginative ways—presented with both ingenuity and honesty; and at the same time available to the expert with full and up-to-date explanations of the methods used. We should like to see much more explicit attention to margins of error, and the design of special experiments to discover and determine errors. We should like to see a less wooden approach to the public—better-designed forms, better-phrased explanations, the avoidance of overlapping, and an effort to show that the public *gets* as well as *gives* something of value.

Above all, we would like to see more conscious thought given to the balance of effort and value received. Is it worth while for the Admiralty to spend public money obtaining returns of shipbuilding when these are already obtained by Lloyd's Register? Does the accuracy and value of employment statistics justify their monthly publication in great detail, or could they appear quarterly? Can resources used for purposes such as these be re-deployed so that the yawning gap in inventory statistics can be filled? Questions like this are important not only because the statistical resources immediately to hand are limited, but because the chances of justifying the employment of more money and personnel depend on showing that the statistical services give 'value for money'. We do not see how any convincing case can be made on such a matter unless somewhere the statistical services are being looked at as a whole, and the importance of their various parts weighed one against another. If our particular solution of the problem, in the last chapter, is unacceptable, we hope at least that the Central Statistical Office will be so strengthened that its staff can raise their heads from the mass of day-to-day work which encumbers their desks, and examine the wider view.

BIBLIOGRAPHY

I. OFFICIAL PUBLICATIONS

A. BRITISH GOVERNMENT PUBLICATIONS: PERIODICAL

(All published by Her Majesty's Stationery Office unless shown otherwise)

[1] *Agricultural Statistics, United Kingdom,* Parts I and II (Agricultural Departments), annual.

[2] *Agricultural Statistics, England and Wales,* Parts I and II (Ministry of Agriculture and Fisheries), annual.

[3] *Agricultural Statistics (Scotland)* (Department of Agriculture for Scotland), annual.

[4] *Agriculture, Monthly Report of the Ministry of* (Northern Ireland).

[5] *Annual Abstract of Statistics* (Central Statistical Office).

[6] *Annual Report of the Registrar-General for Scotland.*

[7] *Annual Report of the Registrar-General for Northern Ireland.*

[8] *Annual Review and Fixing of Farm Prices* (Command Paper). Reference to 1951 issue, Cmd. 8239, unless otherwise stated.

[9] *Annual Statement of the Trade of the United Kingdom* (Customs and Excise Department).

[10] *Appropriation accounts: Air Services* (Air Ministry).
          Army (War Office).
          Civil (Treasury).
          Navy (Admiralty).
(House of Commons Papers), annual. Also for Northern Ireland.

[11] *Balance of Payments, United Kingdom* (Command Papers), half-yearly.
References to:
  [11a] *United Kingdom Balance of Payments, 1946 to 1950,* Cmd. 8065, October 1950.
  [11b] *United Kingdom Balance of Payments, 1949 to 1952 (No. 2),* Cmd. 8808, April 1953.

[12] *Board of Trade Journal,* weekly.

[13] *Census of Population (England and Wales) Preliminary Report,* 1951 (and ten-yearly) (General Register Office).

[14] *Census of Population (Scotland) Preliminary Report,* 1951 (and ten-yearly) (General Registry Office, Edinburgh).

[15] *Census of Population Reports* (England and Wales, Scotland, Northern Ireland) (General Register Office, General Registry Office, Registrar-General), ten-yearly.

[16] *Census of Production Reports* (Great Britain) (Board of Trade) for 1907, 1912, 1924, 1930, 1935, 1946 (partial), 1948, and annually.

[17] *Census of Production Reports* (Northern Ireland) (Ministry of Commerce) for 1930, 1935, 1949, and annually.

[18] *Defence, Statement on* (Command Paper), annual.

[19] *Economic Survey:*

1947	Cmd. 7046	1951	Cmd. 8195
1948	Cmd. 7344	1952	Cmd. 8509
1949	Cmd. 7647	1953	Cmd. 8800
1950	Cmd. 7915		

[20] *Estimates: Air* (Air Ministry).   *Army* (War Office).
          Civil (Treasury).   *Navy* (Admiralty).
          (House of Commons Papers), annual. Also for Northern Ireland.
[21] *Financial Statement* (Statement of Revenue and Expenditure as laid before the House by the Chancellor of the Exchequer when opening the Budget) (Treasury), annual. Also for Northern Ireland.
[22] *Finance Accounts of the United Kingdom* (Treasury), annual. Also for Northern Ireland.
[23] *Guide to Current Official Statistics of the United Kingdom*, annual, published 1922–1938.
[24] *Housing Summary for Great Britain* (Ministry of Housing and Local Government), monthly.
[25] *Housing Return for England and Wales* (Ministry of Housing and Local Government), quarterly.
[26] *Housing Return for Scotland* (Department of Health for Scotland), quarterly.
[27] *Inland Revenue Report*, Report of the Commissioners of H.M. Inland Revenue, annual.
[28] *Journal of the Ministry of Agriculture.*
[29] *Local Government Financial Statistics, England and Wales* (Ministry of Housing and Local Government), annual.
[30] *Local Taxation Returns*, Northern Ireland, annual.
[31] *London Gazette*, twice weekly.
[32] *Ministry of Labour Gazette*, monthly.
[33] *Monthly Digest of Statistics* (Central Statistical Office).
[34] *National Income and Expenditure*, annual.
          References to:
          [34a] Cmd. 8203, 1951.
          [34b] Preliminary estimates for 1951, Cmd. 8486, 1952.
          [34c] *National Income and Expenditure, 1946–1951* (Central Statistical Office), 1952.
          [34d] Preliminary estimates for 1952, Cmd. 8803, 1953.
[35] *Overseas Investment, United Kingdom* (published by the Bank of England), annual.
[36] *Quarterly Return of births, deaths and marriages and infectious diseases* (England and Wales, Scotland, Northern Ireland), (Registrars-General).
[37] *Quarterly Statistical Statement of costs of production, etc.* (coal industry) (now published by the National Coal Board).
[38] *Rates and Rateable Values in England and Wales* (Ministry of Housing and Local Government), annual.
[39] *Rates in Scotland* (Scottish Home Department), annual.
[40] *Registrar General's Statistical Review of England and Wales*, Parts I and II, annual.
[41] *Registry of Ships* (Registrar-General of Shipping and Seamen), monthly.
[42] *Report on Health and Local Government Administration, Northern Ireland* (Ministry of Health), annual.
[43] *Report on Overseas Trade* (Board of Trade), monthly.
[44] *Return of Mechanically-Propelled Vehicles* (Ministry of Transport), quarterly (and annual volume).
[45] *Statistical Digest of the Ministry of Fuel and Power*, annual.
[46] *Summary Table of the Statistical Return of the Railways of Great Britain* (Ministry of Transport), annual, to 1947.
[47] *Tables relating to Employment and Unemployment in Great Britain* (Ministry of Labour and National Service), annual.
[48] *Trade and Navigation Accounts* (Board of Trade), monthly.

[49] *Ulster Year Book* (Registrar-General, Northern Ireland), three-yearly.
[50] *Weekly Return of births, deaths and infectious diseases* (England and Wales, Scotland, Northern Ireland), (Registrars-General).
[51] *Weekly Statistical Statement of the Ministry of Fuel and Power.*

B. BRITISH GOVERNMENT PUBLICATIONS: OCCASIONAL

'Barlow report': see *Distribution of the Industrial Population* [56].
[52] *Britain's Shops* (Board of Trade), 1952.
[53] *Census of Great Britain, 1951, 1% Sample Tables* (General Register Office, etc.), 1952.
[54] *Census Reports of Great Britain, 1801 to 1931*, Guides to Official Sources No. 2, 1951.
[55] *Distribution of Industry Act, 1945.*   [55a] *Distribution of Industry Act, 1950.*
[56] *Distribution of the Industrial Population*, Report of the Royal Commission on the (Barlow report), Cmd. 6153, 1940.
[57] *Distribution of Industry*, Cmd. 7540, 1948.
[58] *Employment Policy*, Cmd. 6527, 1944.
[59] *Fuel and Power Resources*, Report of the Committee on National Policy for the Use of (Ridley report), Cmd. 8647, 1952.
'Girdwood reports': see *House-Building* [61].
[60] *Government Statistical Services* (Central Statistical Office), 1953.
[61] *House-Building, Cost of:* Reports of the Committee on the Cost of House-building (England and Wales) (Girdwood reports) (Ministry of Housing and Local Government; formerly Ministry of Health):
                              First Report   1948.
                              Second Report   1950.
                              Third Report   1952.
[62] *Interim Index of Industrial Production*, Studies in Official Statistics No. 1 (Central Statistical Office), 1949.
[62a] *Index of Industrial Production*, Studies in Official Statistics No. 2 (Central Statistical Office), 1952.
[63] *Index of Retail Prices, Report on the working of the*, Cmd. 8481, 1952.
[64] *Industrial Relations Handbook*, Supplement No. 2 (Interim Index of Retail Prices) (Ministry of Labour and National Service), 1948.
[65] *Interdepartmental Committee on Economic and Social Research* (North Committee), Report.
       References to:
       [65a] Cmd. 7537, 1948.
       [65b] Cmd. 8091, 1950.
[66] *Labour Statistics*, Guides to Official Sources No. 1, 1950.
[67] *Migration, Internal*, Mary P. Newton and James R. Jeffery, General Register Office, 1951.
[68] *National Farm Survey of England and Wales: A Summary Report* (Ministry of Agriculture and Fisheries), 1946.
       Newton and Jeffery, see *Migration* [67].
       'North Committee', see *Interdepartmental Committee* [65].
       'Ridley Committee', see *Fuel and Power Resources* [59].
[69] *Standard Industrial Classification* (Central Statistical Office), 1948.
[70] *Statistical Digest of the War* (Central Statistical Office), 1951.
[71] *Town and Country Planning, 1943–1951*, Cmd. 8204, 1951.

C. Foreign Government Publications

[72] *Balance of International Payments of the United States, 1946–1948* (U.S. Department of Commerce), Washington, U.S. Government Printing Office, 1950.

[73] *Historical Statistics of the United States* (U.S. Bureau of the Census), Washington, U.S. Government Printing Office, 1949.

[74] *National Income, 1929–1950* (U.S. Department of Commerce), Washington, U.S. Government Printing Office, 1951.

[75] *Statistical Abstract of Ireland* (Central Statistics Office), Dublin, Stationery Office, 1951.

[76] *Statistical Organisation in Canada* (Dominion Bureau of Statistics), Ottawa, 1951 (mimeographed).

[77] *Statistical Services of the United States Government*, Washington, U.S. Government Printing Office, 1951.

[78] *Survey of Current Business* (U.S. Department of Commerce), Washington, U.S. Government Printing Office, monthly (weekly supplement).

D. Publications of International Agencies

[79] *Balance of Payments Manual*, Washington, International Monetary Fund, 2nd ed., 1950.

[80] *Economic Survey of Europe, 1951*, Research and Planning Division, Economic Commission for Europe, Geneva, United Nations, 1952.

E. Publications of Public Corporations

[81] *British Transport Commission, Annual Report.*

[82] *Coal Figures*, National Coal Board, monthly (discontinued 1953).

[83] *Plan for Coal*, National Coal Board, 1950.
Quarterly statistical statement of costs of production, etc. (coal industry): see [37].

[84] *Transport Statistics*, British Transport Commission, monthly.

[85] *Ulster Transport Authority, Annual Report.*

II. BOOKS AND ARTICLES

[86] Allen, R. G. D., 'Statistics of the Balance of Payments', *Economic Journal*, vol. LXI, no. 241, March 1951.

[87] Anonymous, *The Second Book of Samuel (The Holy Bible)*, chapter 24.

[88] Barna, T., 'The Interdependence of the British Economy', *Journal of the Royal Statistical Society*, series A, vol. CXV, 1952, part I.

[89] Bowley, Sir A. L. (on the wage index), *London and Cambridge Economic Service:*
    [89a] *Special Memorandum* no. 28, 1929.
    [89b] *Bulletin*, January 1944.
    [89c] *Special Memorandum* no. 50, 1947.

[90] Cairncross, A. K. and Meier, R. L., 'New Industries and Economic Development in Scotland', *Three Banks Review*, no. 14, June 1952.

[91] Carter, C. F., 'Index Numbers of the Real Product of the United Kingdom', *Journal of the Royal Statistical Society*, series A, vol. CXV, 1952, part I.

[92] Chapman, Agatha L., assisted by Rose Knight, *Wages and Salaries in the United Kingdom, 1920–1938*, National Institute of Economic and Social Research and Department of Applied Economics, Cambridge, Cambridge University Press, 1953.

[93] Chester, D. N. (ed.), *Lessons of the British War Economy*, National Institute of Economic and Social Research, Economic and Social Studies X, Cambridge University Press, 1951.

[94] Copeland, M. A., in *The American Statistician* (see [118]), vol. 2, 1948, no. 3.

[95] Giffen, R., *Evidence to the Royal Commission on the Depression of Trade and Industry*, 7 October 1885, London, H.M.S.O., 1885.

[96] Gray, P. G. and Corlett, T., 'Sampling for the Social Survey', *Journal of the Royal Statistical Society*, series A, vol. CXIII, 1950, part II.

[97] Hammond, R. J., *Food* (History of the Second World War, United Kingdom Civil Series, ed. W. K. Hancock), London, H.M.S.O., 1951.

[98] Hansen, M. H. and Long, C. D., in *The American Statistician* (see [118]), vol. 6, no. 1, 1952.

[99] Isserlis, L., 'Tramp Shipping, Cargoes and Freights', *Journal of the Royal Statistical Society*, series A, vol. CI, 1938, part I.

[100] Jackson, E. F., in *Income and Wealth, Series I* (p. 140), published for the International Association for Research in Income and Wealth by Bowes and Bowes, Cambridge, 1951.

[101] Kendall, M. G., 'The U.K. Mercantile Marine and its Contribution to the Balance of Payments', *Journal of the Royal Statistical Society*, series A, vol. CXIII, 1950, part I.

[102] Kendall, M. G. (ed.), *The Sources and Nature of the Statistics of the United Kingdom*, vol. 1, published by Oliver and Boyd for the Royal Statistical Society, London and Edinburgh, 1952.

[103] Keynes, J. M., 'Alfred Marshall, 1842–1924', *Economic Journal*, vol. XXXIV, no. 135, September 1924: reprinted in *Memorials of Alfred Marshall*, ed. A. C. Pigou, London, Macmillan, 1925, and in *Essays in Biography*, by J. M. Keynes, London, Macmillan, 1933.

[104] Linnenberg, C. C., Jr., in *The American Statistician* (see [118]), vol. 3, nos. 2, 3, 1949.

[105] Lomax, K. S., 'Coal Production Functions for Great Britain', *Journal of the Royal Statistical Society*, series A, vol. CXIII, 1950, part III.

[106] Mills, F. C. and Long, C. D., *The Statistical Agencies of the Federal Government*, New York, National Bureau of Economic Research, 1949.

[107] Morgenstern, O., *On the Accuracy of Economic Observations*, Princeton, N.J., Princeton University Press, 1950.

[108] Conference on Research in Income and Wealth, *Studies in Income and Wealth*, vol. 13, New York, National Bureau of Economic Research, 1951.

[109] Palca, H. and Davies, I. G. R., 'Earnings and Conditions of Employment in Agriculture', *Journal of the Royal Statistical Society*, series A, vol. CXIV, 1951, part I.

[110] Prest, A. R., 'National Income of the United Kingdom, 1870–1946', *Economic Journal*, vol. LVIII, no. 229, March 1948.

[111] Ramsbottom, E. C., 'The Course of Wage Rates in the United Kingdom, 1921–1934', *Journal of the Royal Statistical Society*, series A, vol. XCVIII, 1935, part IV.

[112] Reddaway, W. B., 'Movements in the Real Product of the United Kingdom, 1946–1949', *Journal of the Royal Statistical Society*, series A, vol. CXIII, 1950, part IV.

[113] Rice, S., in the *American Political Science Review*, vol. 34, 1940, p. 481.
[114] Rowntree, B. Seebohm, *Poverty: A Study of Town Life*, London, Macmillan, 1901.
[115] Rowntree, B. Seebohm and Lavers, G. R., *Poverty and the Welfare State*, London, Longmans, 1951.
[116] Royal Statistical Society, *Memorandum on Official Statistics*, 1943 (also in the *Journal of the Royal Statistical Society*, series A, vol. CVI, 1943, part II).
[117] Tukey, J. W., in *The American Statistician* (see [118]), vol. 3, nos. 1, 2, 1949.

III. NON-GOVERNMENT PERIODICALS
(General References)

[118] *The American Statistician*, American Statistical Association, Washington, 5 times a year.
[119] *British Iron and Steel Federation Monthly Statistical Bulletin*, London.
[120] *British Iron and Steel Federation Statistical Year Book (United Kingdom)*, London.
[121] *Bulletin of the Oxford University Institute of Statistics*, Oxford, Basil Blackwell, monthly.
[122] *Journal of the Royal Statistical Society*, annual article on Wholesale Prices.
[123] *Lloyd's Register Shipbuilding Returns*, London, quarterly.
[124] *London and Cambridge Economic Service Bulletin*, London, quarterly. Published in *The Times Review of Industry* from March 1952.
[125] *Moody's Services*, London (loose-leaf stock exchange, company and industrial records).
[126] *Records and Statistics*, supplement to *The Economist*, London, weekly. Publication ceased, end of June 1953.
[127] *The Financial Times* newspaper, London, daily.
[128] *The Times* newspaper, London, daily.

REFERENCE TABLE OF PRINCIPAL BRITISH ECONOMIC STATISTICS AND THEIR SOURCES

The table below gives only a selection of British statistics important for economic purposes. They are in the order used in the *Annual Abstract of Statistics*. Below each main heading in the left-hand column are shown the names of the departments primarily responsible for official statistics under that heading, and references to general descriptive publications. Under the heading 'Where published' is shown, first the name of the publication in which the series appears earliest, and secondly (in most cases) a second convenient source. The same series may also appear, with more or less detail, in several other publications not shown here. Under 'Approximate time-lag' is shown the interval between the end of the period to which the figures relate, and the usual date of first publication. In the final column appear notes about detail and coverage, and also the starting-date for series which have only recently become available. Most series for which a starting-date does not appear can be carried back at least to 1930, but often with changes of definition, coverage and source which are too complicated to enumerate here.

Further information about sources can be found in [23] for pre-war years, in [54] and [66], and in the 'Index of Sources' at the end of the *Annual Abstract of Statistics* [5]. There is a schedule of areas of departmental responsibility for the collection of statistics, and a list of principal sources, at the end of [60]. For brevity, four of the principal sources have been referred to as follows:

M   *Monthly Digest of Statistics* [33].
A   *Annual Abstract of Statistics* [5].
T   *Board of Trade Journal* [12].
L   *Ministry of Labour Gazette* [32].

We should like to express our thanks to Mrs M. Robson, who prepared the preliminary draft of this table. It has been corrected, as carefully as possible, up to the time of going to press; but readers should remember that changes are frequent.

G.B. = Great Britain.   E/W = England and Wales.
N.I. = Northern Ireland.   S.I.C. = Standard Industrial Classification [69].

Table 7. *Principal British economic*

Subject	Series	Where published
POPULATION AND VITAL STATISTICS (Registrars-General for England and Wales, Scotland and Northern Ireland) (see [54])	Estimated total population	M *Registrar General's Statistical Review* (E/W), *Annual Report* (Scotland), *Annual Report* (N.I.), [40, 6, 7]
	Enumerated total population	*Census Preliminary Reports* [13, 14] (E/W, Scotland, N.I.) *Census of Great Britain, 1951, 1% Sample Tables* [53]
	Births, deaths	*Weekly Return of births, deaths and infectious diseases* (large towns only) (E/W, Scotland, N.I.) [50] M
	Marriages	M *Quarterly Return of births, deaths and marriages and infectious diseases* (E/W, Scotland, N.I.) [36]
PASSENGER MOVEMENTS ACROSS U.K. FRONTIERS (Board of Trade (G.B.), Ministry of Commerce (N.I.))	Passenger movements by sea and air	T A
LABOUR STATISTICS (Ministry of Labour and National Service (G.B.), Ministry of Labour and National Insurance (N.I.)) (see [66] and Ainsworth in Kendall [102], p. 75)	Employment (G.B.)	L M
	Unemployment	L M
	Working days lost through industrial disputes	L M
	Trade Union membership	L A
	Wage rates: official index	L M
	Wage rates: Sir Arthur Bowley's index	*Bulletin, London and Cambridge Economic Service* (in *The Times Review of Industry*, quarterly) [124]
	Weekly earnings: manufacturing and certain other industries (in a particular week)	L M
	Weekly earnings: Coal mining (G.B.)	*Quarterly Statistical Statement of costs, etc. of collieries* [37]
	Railway service (G.B.)	L *British Transport Commission Report* [81]

Frequency of series	Approximate time-lag	Notes
Half-yearly	3–4 months (*de facto*) 5 months (total)	Totals for the three divisions, by sexes. (Age-distribution in M after about 6 months. Fuller detail, with regions and administrative areas, in second sources after 18 months to 2 years)
10-yearly	3 months (N.I. 6 months)	Totals for administrative areas. (Fuller detail in second source, after 15–18 months. Census Final Reports appear after several years)
Weekly	1–2 weeks	See also, for comprehensive figures, *Quarterly Return of births, deaths and marriages and infectious diseases* [36], and annual *Review* or *Report* [40, 6, 7]. Quarterly figures appear first in M (after 2 months), for the four countries
Quarterly	1 month (Scotland), 3 months (N.I.), 4 months (E/W)	—
Quarterly (published half-yearly)	3 months (from half year)	By type of transport and (immediate) destination. Permanent migrants (outside Europe) by starting point or destination: visitors by nationality. Excludes movement across land frontier with Republic of Ireland, for which see [75]
Monthly	2 months (press release 4–5 weeks)	Total manpower by sex and by 18 industry groups; numbers of insured employees in employment by sex and by S.I.C. industries. Regional data in [47]. Tables exclude Northern Ireland, for which *total* insured (including unemployed) given annually in L: see also [49]. All series start July 1948; previous manpower series from 1938 (see L and [70]); previous series for insured employees in L
Monthly	6 weeks (press release 2–3 weeks)	By sex, region and industry and distinguishing those temporarily stopped. Series from July 1948; previous series in L
Monthly	1 month	By industry
Yearly	11 months	By sex, 28 industry groups, 11 size groups: Unions with head office in the U.K., including membership in Republic of Ireland
Monthly	1 month	All workers, men, women, juveniles. From June 1947: previous versions from 1900, 1914, 1924, 1939. See Ramsbottom [111]
Monthly	7 weeks	Constituent series shown. Available for 1913 and continuously from 1919. See Bowley [89]
Half-yearly	5–6 months	All workers, men, youths, women, girls, and by industries. From 1940 (classification changed 1948): also 1931, 1935, and 1938
Quarterly	4 months	By class of worker
Yearly	11 months	By class of worker

Table 7 (*continued*)

Subject	Series	Where published
LABOUR STATISTICS (*continued*)	Weekly earnings (*continued*) Dock labour Hours worked in a particular week, manufacturing and certain other industries	L L
PRODUCTION INDEX* (Central Statistical Office)	Index of Industrial Production	M T
	Index of Real Product	*Bulletin, London and Cambridge Economic Service* [**124**]
CENSUS OF PRODUCTION (Board of Trade (G.B.), Ministry of Commerce (N.I.)) (See Leak in Kendall [**102**], p. 1)	Gross and net output, number and remuneration of operatives and other staff, etc.	*Census of Production Reports* (G.B. and N.I.) [**16, 17**] T
FUEL AND POWER PRODUCTION (Ministry of Fuel and Power (G.B.)) (see George, p. 87, and Daniel, p. 199, in Kendall [**102**])	Coal production	*Weekly Statistical Statement* [**51**] (to press, from 9 September 1947) M
	Coal consumption	*Weekly Statistical Statement* [**51**] M
	Coal stocks	*Weekly Statistical Statement* [**51**] M
	Coal: productivity	*Weekly Statistical Statement* [**51**] M
	Gas production (G.B.)	*Weekly Statistical Statement* [**51**] M
	Electricity production (G.B.)	*Weekly Statistical Statement* [**51**] M
IRON AND STEEL PRODUCTION (Ministry of Supply (G.B.)) (see Shone in Kendall [**102**], p. 151)	Iron ore production	*BISF Bulletin* [**119**] M
	Pig iron production	*BISF Bulletin* [**119**] M
	Steel production	*BISF Bulletin* [**119**] M
	Finished steel deliveries	*BISF Bulletin* [**119**] M
BUILDING AND CONSTRUCTION (Ministry of Works (G.B.): Ministry of Housing and Local Government (E/W): Department of Health, Scotland: Ministry of Health and Local Government (N.I.))	Value of output (G.B.)	M
	Housing accommodation provided (G.B.) (new permanent and temporary houses, conversions, etc.)	M *Housing Summary* [**24**]
	Permanent houses completed (N.I.)	M
SHIPBUILDING (Admiralty)	Merchant ships laid down, under construction, completed	M

* References to individual production series are not given except for fuel and power, iron and see T for textile production.

Table 7 (*continued*)

Frequency of series	Approximate time-lag	Notes
Half-yearly	5–6 months	From 1943
Half-yearly	5–6 months	As earnings
Monthly	2 months (some Orders up to 5 months)	Yearly from 1948 and monthly from January 1950: described [62a]. Previous index, described [62], from January 1946. Both by S.I.C. Orders. Pre-war index in T, running to August 1939. Many constituent series of the index appear in M and A
Yearly	8 months	Mainly by S.I.C. Orders: from 1946. Details in Carter [91]
Yearly	See notes	Census taken for 1907, 1912, 1924, 1930, 1935, 1946 (certain industries), 1948 (G.B.), 1949 and then annually: similar information for 1933, 1934, 1937. Preliminary reports (G.B.) published in T over a period, after about $1\frac{1}{2}$ years: final reports for 1948 census 3–4 years, 1949 $2\frac{1}{2}$–$3\frac{1}{2}$ years: 1949 N.I. Census 2 years, 1950 N.I. Census $1\frac{1}{2}$ years. See Leak in Kendall [102], p. 1
Weekly	3 days	Deep-mined and opencast. For detail see monthly *Coal Figures* [82] and *Ministry of Fuel and Power Statistical Digest* (yearly) [45]
Weekly	10 days	Total: detail by main classes of consumer, monthly in M and sources [82, 45]
Weekly	10 days	Total: detail by main classes of holder, monthly in M and sources [82, 45]
Weekly	10 days	Output per man-shift, overall and at coal face
Weekly	4 days	—
Weekly	4 days	—
Monthly	1 month	By type and area
Monthly	1 month	By quality and district
Monthly	1 month	By quality, process and district
Monthly	2 months	By types
Quarterly	2 months	Partly by type of work, partly by agency. From 1941 (partial), 1946
Monthly	1 month	New houses, conversions, requisitionings, etc. by authorities responsible for building. See also *Housing Returns* (E/W, Scotland: quarterly) [25, 26]
Monthly	1 month	—
Monthly	1 month	Tankers and others. From 1940 (year), 1941 (quarterly), 1944 (monthly): see [70] and M.

steel, shipbuilding, building, and agriculture; they can usually be traced through M or A, but

Table 7 (continued)

Subject	Series	Where published
SHIPBUILDING (continued)	Merchant ships—keel laid, launched, completed, under construction (2 stages)	Lloyd's Register Shipbuilding Returns [123]
AGRICULTURE (Ministry of Agriculture and Fisheries (E/W), Department of Agriculture (Scotland), Ministry of Agriculture (N.I.)) (see Britton and Hunt in Kendall [102], p. 35)	Crops harvested (22 types)	M U.K.: Agricultural Statistics [1]
	Cattle, sheep, pigs—numbers (16 types)	M U.K.: Agricultural Statistics [1]
	Poultry—numbers	M U.K.: Agricultural Statistics [1]
EXTERNAL TRADE (Board of Trade (G.B.), Ministry of Commerce (N.I.)) (see Maizels in Kendall [102], p. 17)	Imports, exports, re-exports: (i) Values	Trade and Navigation Accounts [48] Report on Overseas Trade [43]
	(ii) Physical quantities (where recorded)	Trade and Navigation Accounts [48]
	(iii) Volume index numbers (total imports, retained imports, U.K. exports)	T Report on Overseas Trade [43]
	(iv) Average value index numbers (as (iii))	T Report on Overseas Trade [43]
	(v) Import and export price index numbers	T M
	Tramp shipping freight rates index	Newspapers (e.g. The Times [128]) M
BALANCE OF PAYMENTS (Treasury)	Details of current and 'investment and financing' accounts	White Papers [11] A
	Gold and dollar reserves	Press release Balance of Payments White Papers [11]
WHOLESALE AND RETAIL TRADE (Board of Trade (G.B.), Ministry of Commerce (N.I.), Ministry of Food)	Wholesale textile houses—sales and stocks (value) (G.B.)	T M
	Numbers of shops and service trade establishments (G.B.)	Britain's Shops [52] A
	Values of retail sales (also stocks for clothing and footwear, shops of type (i)) (G.B.): (i) Department stores, multiple shops and retail co-operative societies	T M
	(ii) 'Independent' traders	T M
	Numbers of meals served in catering establishments	A
TRANSPORT (Ministry of Transport (G.B.), Ministry of Commerce (N.I.); also Board of Trade and Ministry of Civil Aviation) (See Kendall [102], pp. 267, 279)	Merchant vessels on U.K. register (gross tons)	Registry of Ships [41] M
	Entrances and clearances of shipping at U.K. ports (net tons)	Trade and Navigation Accounts [48] T

Table 7 (*continued*)

Frequency of series	Approximate time-lag	Notes
Quarterly	1 month	By type, size group and district
Yearly	2–3 months from harvest	Areas for 36 uses
Quarterly	3 months	March figures omitted for sheep
Half-yearly	3 months	—
Monthly	3 weeks (press release 2–3 weeks)	By commodities, and principal countries for major commodities. Further detail and country breakdown in *Annual Statement of Trade* [9]
Monthly	3 weeks	—
Quarterly	6 weeks	For totals and main classes and groups (base year changed periodically)
Quarterly	6 weeks	As (iii)
Monthly	1 month	For totals and 3 subdivisions of each (base year changed frequently; available from January 1945, with annual figures to 1938)
Monthly	2 weeks	From 1948–mid 1953, revised version January 1952 to date (see Kendall [101]); similar index available pre-war (see Isserlis [99])
Half-yearly (some quarterly figures)	3½ months	Details by 6 areas: from 1946. Some pre-war estimates in T
Monthly	2–3 days	Quarterly before January 1952: yearly before 1946
Monthly	5 weeks	From Bank of England and Wholesale Textile Association: starts 1938
See notes	See notes	Preliminary enumeration for Census of Distribution purposes; will presumably be available, together with data from the Census, at intervals of a few years
Monthly	5 weeks (press release 4 weeks)	By area and type of shop and type of goods sold
Monthly	5 weeks (press release 4 weeks)	From 1947: by type of goods sold
Yearly (single month)	9–12 months	By type of establishment, all meals and 'main' meals. From 1942
Monthly	1 month (in M)	By port, size, construction, method of propulsion
Monthly	3 weeks	By nationality and trading area: T gives figures by ports and port areas

Table 7 (*continued*)

Subject	Series	Where published
TRANSPORT (*continued*)	Airways passenger-miles and mail and freight ton-miles	M A
	Road vehicles: Licences current (G.B.)	M *Return of Mechanically-Propelled Vehicles* [44]
	New registrations (G.B.)	M
	Railways: Passenger journeys originating (G.B.)	M *Transport Statistics* [84]
	Passenger-miles (G.B.)	Financial and statistical accounts of the British Transport Commission in [81] A
	Freight ton-miles (G.B.)	M *Transport Statistics* [84]
	Passenger journeys and freight tonnage (N.I.)	A
PUBLIC FINANCE (Central Government) (Treasury and Ministry of Finance (N.I.))	Revenue (actual receipts)	*London Gazette* [31] *Finance Accounts of the United Kingdom* [22]
	Expenditure (actual issues)	*London Gazette* [31] *Appropriation Accounts* [10]
	Revenue (expected)	*Financial Statement* [21]
	Expenditure (expected)	*Financial Statement* [21] Departmental estimates [20]
	National Debt outstanding	*Financial Statement* [21] *Finance Accounts of the United Kingdom* [22]
PUBLIC FINANCE (Local Government) (Ministry of Housing and Local Government (E/W), Scottish Home Department, Ministry of Health and Local Government (N.I.))	Income and expenditure of local authorities: E/W	*Local Government Financial Statistics* [29]
	Scotland	A
	N.I.	*Local Taxation Returns* [30]
NATIONAL INCOME AND EXPENDITURE (Central Statistical Office)	Gross national product, expenditure, and numerous related statistics	*National Income and Expenditure* [34] A
	Consumer expenditure at current market prices and at constant prices	M
BANKING, ETC. (Bank of England, London Clearing Bankers, British Bankers' Association, Bankers' Clearing House, National Savings Committee)	Currency circulation with the public	M
	Bank deposits, and assets (by type) (London clearing banks)	M
	Bank advances (G.B.) (by type of borrower)	*Financial Times* [127] M
	Bank clearings, London and provincial	M

Table 7 (*continued*)

Frequency of series	Approximate time-lag	Notes
Monthly	3 months	Internal and external services distinguished
Quarterly	3 months	By type of vehicle: annual volume [44] gives detail by licensing authority and numerous types
Monthly	3 months	—
Monthly	3 months	By type of ticket
Yearly	6 months	Before 1948 see [46]
Monthly	2 months	—
Yearly	9–12 months	Includes whole of Great Northern Railway (Ireland) and excludes minor cross-border lines. See also [49]
Weekly	1 week	Detail in *Finance Accounts*, yearly, after 6 months. See also A
Weekly	1 week	Detail in *Appropriation Accounts*, yearly, after 1 year. See also A
Yearly	(At Budget)	—
Yearly	(At Budget)	—
	(2–3 months before Budget)	
Yearly	1 week	—
Yearly	2 years	See also A, and Rating returns [38]
Yearly	3 years	—
Yearly	3 years	—
Yearly	3 months (preliminary)	Certain quarterly estimates in *Bulletin of the Oxford University Institute of Statistics* [121]
	9 months (in full)	Official estimates from 1938 (varying detail)
Quarterly	2–3 months	13 subdivisions. From 1938
Monthly	1 month	—
Monthly	6 weeks (press release 2–3 weeks)	—
Quarterly	3 weeks	—
Monthly	1 month	—

Table 7 (*continued*)

Subject	Series	Where published
BANKING, ETC. (*continued*)	'Small' savings—total outstanding	M
PRICES (Board of Trade, Ministry of Labour, Ministry of Agriculture, Bank of England, etc., and corresponding departments)	Import and export prices	See under 'External Trade'
	Commodity price index numbers	T
	Industrial material (i.e. input) price index numbers	T
		M
	Agricultural fertilizer price index (E/W)	M
	Agricultural feeding stuffs price indices: also store cattle, sheep and pigs (E/W)	A
		Agricultural Statistics [2]
	Industrial output price index numbers	T
		M
	Agricultural output price index numbers (E/W)	M
		Agricultural Statistics [2]
	Retail price index numbers	L
		M
	Stock and share price index numbers:	
	Financial Times	*Financial Times* [127]
	Actuaries' Investment Index	*The Economist* supplement [126], or *Financial Times* [127]
		M
	Moody's Equity Price Index	Moody's Services [125]
		London and Cambridge Economic Service Bulletin [124]
	British Government security prices (Bank of England index numbers)	M
	Foreign exchange rates	*Financial Times* [127]
		M

Table 7 (*continued*)

Frequency of series	Approximate time-lag	Notes
Monthly	2 months (weekly press release 1 week)	—
—	—	—
Monthly	2 weeks	Numerous commodities: from various dates, 1945–49. For earlier dates, see *The Economist, J.R.S.S.* [122], etc.
Monthly	2 weeks	5 industry groups: from various dates, 1945–49
Monthly	2 months	—
Yearly	9–12 months	—
Monthly	2 weeks	Numerous industries: from various dates, 1945–49
Monthly	2 months (press release 4–5 weeks)	By types of product: see also full detail in A. See also [3], [4]
Monthly	6 weeks (press release 4–5 weeks)	Re-weighted from January 1952: previous indices from 1947 and 1914. See *London and Cambridge Economic Service* [124]. 9 subdivisions
Daily	1 day	Government securities, fixed interest, industrial ordinary, gold mines, gold developing (from 1950)
Weekly	2 days	22 groups
Monthly	3 weeks	33 groups (not all published in sources shown)
Monthly	1 week	—
Monthly	1 month	Short and medium dated, $3\frac{1}{2}$% War Loan and $2\frac{1}{2}$% Consols, and yields
Daily	1 day	23 centres, 10 forward rates, and cross rates

GENERAL INDEX

INDEX OF PROPOSALS AND SUGGESTIONS

Organization and Methods

A committee to make a regular review of Government economic statistics proposed, 159

More contact between users and providers of statistics desirable, 138–9

Heads of statistical sections not to be regarded simply as technical experts, but to be involved in policy discussions, 153

A greater use of sampling probably advantageous, 157–60

Sample studies of errors needed, 120

A central review of forms desirable, 157

Confidentiality of returns to be limited in scope or time, 134

Better regional statistics needed, 154

An industrial classification of companies to be publicly available, 156

A register of business premises by use to be compiled, 59, 155

Presentation

(The need for more published description, interpretation and comment is frequently noted in the case-studies of Chapters IV–IX.)

More descriptions of methods of estimation needed, 130, 131, 138

'Provisional' estimates to be distinguished, and their origin described, 122, 135

An abstract of historical statistics desirable, 137

Statistical information from all Departments to be released early through the *Board of Trade Journal*, 135, 137

Where a suspected bias is corrected, the correction to be explicitly stated, 120

More detailed discussion of errors needed, 120, 131

Subjective estimates of error desirable when quantitative investigations of error are impossible, 120–1

Examples of new statistical studies which would be useful

Agriculture—new type of annual sample survey of farm accounts, 76–8

Development areas—study of firms' results, 61

Fuel—demand analysis, 46

House-building—continued productivity studies, 27

Housing—examination of scope and presentation of statistics, 30

Housing—national sample investigation of social and economic aspects, 21, 25

Industrial growth of small areas, 60

Labour mobility between firms and industries, 29, 110

Local authorities—special studies of their areas, 25

Migration, internal, 29, 60, 110

Production and productivity studies, 111

Social accounts—quarterly data, 111

Social accounts—study of interrelation of errors, 122

Statistics, general—'efficiency studies', e.g. to get the best combination of accuracy and speed of publication, 160

Printed in the United States
By Bookmasters